16.95

W9-BOB-886

Tips and Traps
When Mortgage
Hunting

Other McGraw-Hill Books by Robert Irwin

Tips and Traps When Buying a Home

Tips and Traps When Selling a Home

Tips and Traps When Buying a Co-Op, Condo, or Townhouse

Tips and Traps for Making Money in Real Estate

Tips and Traps When Renovating Your Home

Tips and Traps for New Home Owners

How to Find Hidden Real Estate Bargains

How to Buy a Home When You Can't Afford It

How to Get Started in Real Estate Investing

Home Buyer's Checklist

Home Seller's Checklist

Home Renovation Checklist

Home Closing Checklist

Buy, Rent, and Sell

Tips and Traps When Mortgage Hunting

Robert Irwin

Third Edition

McGraw-Hill

New York   Chicago   San Francisco   Lisbon   London
Madrid   Mexico City   Milan   New Delhi   San Juan
Seoul   Singapore   Sydney   Toronto

The *McGraw·Hill* Companies

1 2 3 4 5 6 7 8 9 0   FGR/FGR   0 9 8 7 6 5

ISBN 0-07-144892-6

This publication is designed to provide accurate and authoritative information in regard to the subject matter covered. It is sold with the understanding that neither the author nor the publisher is not engaged in rendering legal, accounting, or other professional service. If legal advice or other expert assistance is required, the services of a competent professional person should be sought.
      —From a Declaration of Principles jointly adopted by a Committee of the American Bar Association and a Committee of Publishers and Associations

McGraw-Hill books are available at special quantity discounts to use as premiums and sales promotions, or for use in corporate training programs. For more information, please write to the Director of Special Sales, McGraw-Hill Professional, Two Penn Plaza, New York, NY 10121-2298. Or contact your local bookstore.

 This book is printed on recycled, acid-free paper containing a minimum of 50% recycled, de-inked fiber.

For Marc, who's just starting out in real estate.

Contents

3. Critical Questions to Ask When Getting a Mortgage

Acknowledgments

A grateful thanks to the lending professionals who provided input for this book, especially to Art Jr. of A C Mortgage Services. A special thanks to Jason Benjamin for his work in compiling data, fact-checking, and helping with the organization. And, of course, my endless appreciation to my wife, Rita, who prodded me onward to complete the project.

1

How Do I Get a Purchase Mortgage?

Even if you're totally new to the home purchasing process, it will quickly become clear that almost certainly you will need a mortgage in order to buy a home. With the median price for homes exceeding $200,000 nationwide and $400,000 and much higher on the coasts, few people can afford to pay cash these days. A new mortgage is the rule.

TIP

If you're planning on refinancing instead of buying, you'll also want to check this chapter, as most of the material applies.

But, how does one get a mortgage? How do you get the lowest interest rate? The best terms? The fewest "garbage fees" (unwarranted costs tacked on by lenders and others involved in closing)?

We'll see how it's done by following the example of Leon and Janet, two capable individuals who are buying their first property.

Find the Loan or Find the House?

Leon and Janet were ready for their first home. After living in an apartment for three years, they had saved roughly $10,000. While it wasn't much in terms of a home purchase, they hoped to be able to parley it into enough for a down payment and closing costs. (We'll see how to buy with no cash, shortly.)

A home offered them privacy, security, and the potential for profit. The strong appreciation of real estate in recent years hadn't been lost on them. They wanted to get on that money train as quickly as possible. Besides, down the road they envisioned having a family, so, all in all, a house of their own seemed like a good foundation with which to begin.

Leon suggested they begin looking at homes right away.

Alice's Open House

There were several open houses in their neighborhood. Most were crowded with people, so Janet and Leon really didn't have the opportunity to talk with an agent. However, they did notice that homes in their area seemed to be priced between $200,000 and $300,000. At the third open house, on Pine Street, they were the only lookers at the time, so they spoke with the agent, Alice.

She showed them the house, then very quickly turned the conversation to finances. She seemed to be the sort of person who got right to the point and didn't mince words. She asked, "Have you been preapproved for a mortgage?"

They looked at each other and shook their heads; then Leon began explaining how much money they had. Alice raised her hand and said, "Say no more. I don't need or want to know your personal financial information. What you need to do is to call a lender or a mortgage broker who can get you approved for financing. You'll learn how big a loan and how big a house you can afford. You'll be wasting both of our time until you get that information."

Alice explained that, today, mortgage brokers handled most real estate financing. They represented many lenders; sometimes each broker would have a stable of as many as a hundred or more lenders from which to choose. They could best fit the borrower to the mortgages available.

Alice said that they could easily get qualified by checking with one of the many online mortgage brokers such as eloan.com, lendingtree.com, or mortgage.com. However, she said she preferred dealing with a mortgage broker in person. Alice wrote down the names of two mortgage brokers that she used. She suggested that Leon and Janet call them about financing. When they got that straight, they could come back and see her about a house.

TIP

It's usually easier for a first-time borrower to deal with a live lender. Once you gain experience and know what questions to ask and what to expect, you can shop the Internet for the other loan deals. Use Internet lenders' mortgage calculators to get a quick estimate of your payment.

Al, the Mortgage Broker

When they got home, Janet called a friend who had recently purchased a home and got the name of yet another mortgage broker. Then she called all three. She began by asking them all the same general information, namely:

"How many lenders do you service?

"How long have you been in the business?

"Can you give me a list of satisfied borrowers with whom you've worked in the past few months?"

One mortgage broker said he didn't have time to bother with all these questions because he was so busy. If they wanted to know how much they could afford, just tell him their basic income and he'd calculate it. Janet gave that information to him and he said, "You'll probably be able to get a mortgage of around $220,000." When Janet then persisted about his qualifications, he hung up on her. The other two were more agreeable and provided information.

One broker said she had been in the mortgage business for only a few months and was switching to it from real estate sales. She said she really couldn't yet provide a list of satisfied borrowers, but could provide a list of satisfied home buyers. She seemed anxious to work with Janet and Leon.

The other broker, named Al, said he'd been in the business more than 10 years and had over 50 lenders with whom he worked. When Al learned that Leon and Janet were working with Alice, an old friend, he asked her to fax over a list of six recent borrowers for whom he'd provided mortgages and who had bought through her.

TIP

There are two stages in applying for a mortgage. The first is to find out how big a loan you can get. The second is to get a good mortgage broker who will provide service. Almost anyone (including some online wizards) can give you the maximum loan amount figure. Janet, however, wanted to move right to the second stage and work with the person she felt would give them the best service right from the beginning.

TRAP

Don't be afraid to call references. If people have had good service, they don't mind spreading the good word. And if they have had bad service, they'll be sure to let you know, too. (Just be sure you're not talking to the mortgage broker's brother-in-law!)

Janet began calling people from the middle of the list, and after three calls where each borrower said how satisfied he or she was with Al, Janet figured that she and Leon had their mortgage broker.

She called Al back, and he said he could do the preliminary qualifying work over the phone. But Janet said she wanted to meet him personally, since she expected to get their mortgage through him. Al said he usually didn't meet his clients in person until they had a house under contract and were ready to move forward with a loan. "It's a bit awkward to discuss financing in your home until then," he said.

But Janet said they would make every effort to see that he was comfortable. Besides, they were old-fashioned. They liked to deal face to face with the person with whom they were doing business.

Al hesitated at first, but he finally agreed to do it. He said it was an unusual step for him, but because Alice had recommended him and he got a lot of business through her, and because Janet sounded so nice, he'd make an exception and come over.

The next day, Al showed up at Leon and Janet's home in the evening after they had finished dinner. He was a pleasant man in his forties and told them his story. Originally, as is the case with many mortgage brokers, he had begun by selling real estate. But, he found he didn't like the work. Rather, he preferred the challenge of finding mortgages for people, so he moved into the mortgage brokerage field. He had a real estate license from the state and belonged to the National Association of Mortgage Brokers. And he was eager to help them get a loan to buy a home.

Leon pointed out that they didn't have a lot of money, only about $10,000 saved.

Al noted that this wasn't much, given the price of homes. But in today's lending market, it could be enough. Provided they had good credit and sufficient income, they could hope to get a "nothing-down" loan.

"But," he said, "before we begin, there are a couple of questions I need to ask you. The most basic is, how long do you anticipate living in the house?"

Janet and Leon looked at each other. They hadn't really considered this. "Forever!" Leon said.

"At least 7 or 8 years, maybe 10," said Janet. "Until we have a family and need a bigger place." Leon looked at Janet, but he said nothing.

Al continued, "The reason I ask is because you should decide up front the kind of mortgage you want. There are two basic types. You can get a slightly lower interest rate ARM—adjustable rate mortgage—or a slightly higher fixed rate. With an ARM, the payments can move up if interest rates in general go up. That means that your payment can go up, sometimes as much as 15 percent a year. With a fixed rate, your payment remains constant.

"If you plan on living in the home a long time, the stability of a fixed rate is usually a good idea. If, on the other hand, you plan on selling or refinancing in a short time, sometimes the initially lower interest rate of the ARM can be attractive."

Leon and Janet looked at each other and both said, "fixed rate." They indicated the idea of a constant payment appealed to them.

"That's good," Al said, "because most nothing-down loans, which is what you need, are fixed rate." Then he brought out an application and began filling it out by asking them questions. Most of the questions related to their sources of income and their employment. They quickly answered all his questions.

"How big a loan do you think we can get?" Janet asked.

Al replied, "Based on your income and assuming you have good credit, you should be able to get a fixed-rate nothing-down mortgage of $250,000."

Janet looked surprised and said she had talked with a different mortgage broker and he had told her they could only get $220,000. Al replied that he didn't know about that, but that he had been doing this for a long time and they were certainly at the $250,000 level, provided, as he said, that their credit was okay.

Janet explained they had always paid their bills on time and, as far as she knew, they had no credit problems, so that shouldn't be an issue.

TIP

Today, mortgages are available for most borrowers regardless of many credit situations. Those with worse credit usually have only to pay a higher interest rate or put more money down. Check with a good mortgage broker.

"Good," Al said, "We'll move forward on that basis," and he finished filling out the application, asking them about their bank accounts.

When he was finished, he explained he would submit the application to a lender who would run a credit check on them. The lender would come back with a maximum loan amount and payment preapproval letter.

"When you're ready to make an offer, let me know and I'll draw up a letter based on the lender's preapproval and fax it to you to give to the seller."

"But," Leon protested, "I thought I'd get the letter from you right away. That's what online lenders I've looked at offer."

"Yes," Al said. "I could get the letter to you right away. But, what if you want to buy a house where you're trying to get the buyer to come down on the price and only need a $240,000 mortgage? If your letter says you can qualify for $250,000, that will work against you in trying to get the buyer to drop the price. The buyer will simply look at the letter, see that you can afford to pay more, and stick to his price."

Leon nodded. "So, it's a negotiating tactic." Al nodded. "But, what if we need to make several offers and need several different letters along the way?"

"I'll be happy to oblige each time," said Al. "My motto is service. I'll do my best to serve your needs, even if it means writing up three, four, or more different letters, each suited to each deal that you're doing."

Janet and Leon nodded at each other. They had indeed gotten the right mortgage broker.

TIP

Today, virtually every buyer is preapproved. Buyers compete with one another over their preapprovals. The key to winning is to get the right kind of letter. Savvy sellers will pay more attention to a letter that comes from a lender than one made out by a real estate agent or almost anyone else.

Al further explained that the lender's preapproval letter contained all sorts of technical information including their social security numbers, terms of approval, and loan contingencies. He said he would never show that directly to the seller. Rather, his letter would just contain the essentials the sellers needed to know, including the fact that the letter was based on a lender's preapproval, not just his word.

Al said that before he left, there were a couple more areas he wanted to cover, at least briefly."

"What's that?" Leon asked.

"When you get a mortgage, it's not just the interest rate that counts." Al said, "It's also the points (1 point is 1 percent of the loan) and the terms. Sometimes a loan with a higher interest rate can actually be a better deal in the long run because it has fewer points and better terms. We'll see this clearer when we actually look at loans.

"The next thing to consider is 'PMI.'"

Enter PMI

Janet and Leon looked at each other and laughed. "PMI?" they asked in unison.

"It stands for 'private mortgage insurance,'" Al said. "In order to get a mortgage where you put 20 percent or less down, nearly all lenders require it. It will add about a half a percent or more over your interest rate. The lower the down payment, the higher the PMI."

"That's not good," Janet said. "Do we have to get it?"

"I'm afraid so, in one form or another," Al replied.

"The insurance is for the lender, not you." Al said, "If you don't make your payments and the loan goes into foreclosure, the lender gets paid back its money. You pay for it, but the lender is the one who's insured."

"Is it at least tax deductible?" asked Leon.

"When it's listed as PMI, it's not tax deductible," Al said. "However, some lenders will self-insure and include it in a higher interest rate. Then it is tax deductible."

"That's the way to go." Leon said.

"Maybe," Al replied. "But consider, after a few years with prices appreciating the way they have, your property could be worth far more and your equity might be 20 percent or more of the value. In that case, if it's listed as PMI, you may be able to get the lender to remove it, lowering your payment. (See Chapter 18.) On the other hand, if it's rolled into the mortgage interest rate, there's no removing the PMI no matter how big your equity gets."

"Wow," Leon said. "There are some subtleties, here."

TIP

It is possible to get a high loan-to-value (LTV) without having to get PMI. It's done by getting an 80 percent first mortgage (remember, no PMI is required when the loan is 80 percent or less of LTV) and a second mortgage for up to 20 percent or more. Check into Chapter 2.

Al nodded and said, "Here's one more subtlety—prepayment. Some lenders include a built-in charge in the loan for paying it off early. The penalty can be six months' interest or more! I'm going to put you with a lender who doesn't charge a prepayment fee."

"I can't believe a lender would charge us for paying off a mortgage early!" Janet said. "You'd think they'd be happy to get their money back."

"Believe me," Al said, "Many charge. They do this mainly to discourage you from refinancing to a lower-interest-rate loan. As I said, it's something I don't recommend for my clients."

They both nodded in agreement.

The whole session had taken only about 45 minutes. Leon and Janet signed the application, and Al thanked them and noted that the credit report cost $35. He asked them for a check, but said that if they got a mortgage through him, he would refund the money. Janet wrote out the check.

TIP

Many mortgage brokers will pay for the credit report themselves. However, be wary of a mortgage broker who asks for a big upfront fee to get the loan. Paying that fee locks you in to the broker (go elsewhere and you'll probably forfeit the money), and may result in a higher-cost mortgage down the road. When a broker asks for a big upfront fee, consider doing business elsewhere.

Al also provided them with a booklet prepared by HUD (the federal department of Housing and Urban Development) that explained the mortgage process and spelled out many of their rights when applying for a mortgage. He also said he would provide them with a RESPA (Real Estate Settlement Procedures Act) "good faith estimate," which would detail most of the lender's closing costs, as well as with a Federal Truth-in-Lending Disclosure Statement, which would specify the APR (annual percentage rate) they'd be paying. He said he was required by law to send these to them within three days.

"So," Janet said, "we'll know our closing costs as soon as we get the good faith estimate."

Al smiled and said, "Just keep in mind it's an estimate. I deal with honest lenders and they are within 10 percent of that estimate, as the law requires.

"However," he cautioned, "in a purchase transaction, lots of fees have nothing to do with the lender. For example, the lender relies on industry averages to put down estimates for title and escrow charges. Your actual charges, which are beyond the lender's control, could be far more or less. Further, the lender doesn't know the cost of inspections, prorations, and other things."

TRAP

Do not rely on the good faith estimate form. While it is provided by lenders and intended to give an accurate estimate of closing costs, in recent years these forms have been abused by a few unscrupulous lenders. Ultimate costs have sometimes been significantly higher. Unfortunately, the federal government has been lax in its enforcement of the RESPA rules against these lenders.

Al left with the promise to return in a couple of days. Two days later he was back with the good faith estimate and the APR form, as well as some news.

The Credit Rating

The first thing that Al explained was that Janet and Leon had a 680 "credit score." It was enough to entitle them to some excellent loan programs.

Leon looked puzzled. "What's a credit score?" He asked. "Is that like a credit report?"

"Not exactly," Al replied. He pointed out that the credit report was based on a search of their credit at the three national credit repositories (Experian, TransUnion, and Equifax). The lender contacted a local credit bureau, which contacted each of the three credit repositories and then put together a "merged" report. This pulled all the reports of their credit and then eliminated any duplications. Since each big credit repository represents a different geographical area, this covered all reports of their credit nationwide.

Al explained that this merged report would pick up anything, adverse or favorable, about their credit reported from smaller bureaus around the country. Virtually all lenders, including credit card companies, banks, even utilities and some landlords, report in this fashion. If Leon or Janet had any bad credit, it would show up here.

"If that's a credit *report*," Janet said, "What's a credit *score*?"

Al explained, "Each credit bureau also provides a credit score. The credit report is simply a series of statements about your credit. It needs to be interpreted. To be given a value judgment.

"That's done by credit scoring companies. They analyze factors such as how long you've had credit, how much credit you have, and how well you manage it to come up with a numerical representation of your ability to repay a loan. Generally most use a scale of between 300 and 850. The higher the numerical score, the more likely you are to repay the mortgage, hence the better your chance to be approved for a loan. And the better the loan (meaning a lower interest rate) you're likely to get."

Al pointed out there were many credit scoring companies whose job it was to analyze credit reports. These included CreditXpert, PLUS Score, and FICO (Fair Isaac), the most well known. When provided with three credit scores from each of the three credit repositories, Al said it was his experience that lenders would take either the middle or, occasionally, the lowest score. They would not average the scores out. "Your middle score was 680."

"Is 680 a good score?" Leon asked.

"Actually," Al said, "It's the bottom of good credit. Anything below 680 and you might have the lender asking questions before providing the loan."

"But," Janet replied, "We should have perfect credit. Why wouldn't we get a 700 or even an 800?"

Al replied, "Quite frankly, the credit scoring agencies do most of their work in secret. They'll list the primary factors influencing their report. But, to my eyes, the things they put down, such as a borrower has not had a long enough history of credit when the borrower has 10 years of credit history, often make no sense.

"I simply can't tell you why you have the score you have. Just be happy that your score is high enough for us to move forward without a problem. You'll get a good mortgage."

"But," Leon asked, "Does that 680 score follow us around from now on like a label or tag? Will we run into it every time we want to borrow?"

"Not exactly," Al explained. "It's like a snapshot, a look at your credit in a moment of time. It mostly refers to how much available credit you have and how much of that you have consumed. In the future, depending on how well you use your credit, your score may go up—or down.

"By the way, the lender will run another credit check and credit score just before funding the mortgage, to make sure your credit hasn't changed. If it has, you might not get the loan just before escrow closes. So don't make any big purchases between now and closing, or else it could throw off the ratio of how much credit you have to how much you've used, and adversely affect your score."

TRAP

Don't make a big purchase right before closing on a mortgage. Buying a car, for example, will change the ratio between your available credit and your credit used and could lower your score, thus keeping you from getting the mortgage.

"But," Leon interrupted, "You said our score of 680 is good, so we don't have to worry."

"Right," Al replied, "Not to worry, unless you buy a car or something else big between now and then on credit, which is unlikely, isn't it?"

Leon nodded his head.

TIP

Credit scores mean different things to different companies. Here is an example of typical scoring:

740 and higher	The best credit
700 to 739	Considered excellent credit
680 to 699	Good credit, but the lender may sometimes require extra information from the borrower
600 to 679	Considered risky credit. The borrower may need to pay a higher interest rate to get the loan, and certain loans will be off limits.
300 to 600	Considered poor credit. The borrower may not be able to get institutional financing.

See Chapter 7 for more on credit scoring.

The Mortgage Payment

"Okay," Janet said, "We've settled that we can get a mortgage. Now, just how big will it be and how much will it cost us each month?"

"Right," Al said indicating she had hit the nail on the head with her question. "According to the lender, you can afford a payment of

$2,000 a month, including principal, interest, taxes, and insurance plus homeowner's fees, if any."

"Wow," Leon commented. "That's a big payment!"

"Yes it is," Al said. "But, the numbers don't lie. That's what a lender is willing to loan you."

"You said including taxes and insurance," Janet interrupted. Do those get added into the payment?"

"Yes, they do." Al replied. "That means that when you find the house you're interested in, we'll have to back out the taxes, insurance, and homeowner's fees, if any, to get the actual principal and interest payment. Assuming industry standards, these will cost $500 a month, so you can afford $1,500 for just the mortgage—plus PMI."

"But," Leon asked looking askance, "I don't see how we can make a $2,000 payment every month. Maybe once in a while, but we'd have to cut back on a lot of things to do it. We couldn't eat out every night, or keep up with Janet's horse-riding lessons, or ..."

Al held up his hand. "You're right. If you opt for this maximum payment, it could impact your lifestyle. You might have to sacrifice something in order to make it. That's your decision to make. What's more important, the house or the other things?"

Leon and Janet looked at each other. Then she said, "Okay, our payment will be $2,000 a month, including everything, and we can get a nothing-down $250,000 mortgage, right?"

"The payment will not include everything," Al said. "There will be utilities, phone, TV, garbage, and so on, that's additional. Plus, of course, any repairs and maintenance that's necessary. But yes, the payment and the loan amount are as you said."

TIP

Low to nothing-down loans with the best interest rate and points are generally "conforming loans." That means they "conform" to Fannie Mae and Freddie Mac underwriting loan limits. There is a maximum loan amount which is usually changed every December and which goes into effect in January. The current loan maximum is $359,650. Additionally, in the case of nothing-down financing, the borrower normally must agree to occupy the property to get the loan.

"But, what about closing costs? How are we going to pay for those?" Janet asked.

The Dreaded Closing Costs

"There are always closing costs," Al said. "The only two questions are how much and where the money comes from."

He went on to explain that, as home buyers, Janet and Leon would probably not be responsible for a real estate commission (unless they had a buyer's agent), but they likely would be responsible for the following:

- Points from the lender
- Title insurance and escrow charges that are not lender charges and that the seller does not pay
- Prorations that are not lender charges
- Mortgage fees from the lender

Al said that the current mortgage for which they had qualified had a 1-point origination fee. Since a point was equal to 1 percent of the $250,000 mortgage, that came to $2,500. Additionally, in their locale it was customary to split title insurance and escrow fees between buyer and seller. Their share might be around $2,000.

Prorations, Al explained, meant paying back to the seller any costs that the seller had paid in advance, such as taxes on the property.

And, of course, lenders always tacked on additional fees, most of which went to services they actually performed. Al said the lenders he used had only moderate fees, which shouldn't amount to more than about $1,000.

"Altogether," Al said, "that comes to about $6,000, well within your budget."

"That'll only leave us about $4,000," Leon complained.

"That's good," Al replied. "Lenders like to see that you have at least two months' payments in reserve with a nothing-down loan."

No Closing Cost Mortgages

Janet was shaking her head. She said, "I've heard that it's possible to get a mortgage for no closing costs. Is that true?"

Al nodded. "Indeed it is. Remember, I said that there were always closing costs. It only depends on who pays them. In the case I've outlined, they'd come from your savings. However, there are other avenues to explore."

Al went on to explain that they might be able to have the lender absorb most or all of the closing costs. "In other words, the lender will pay them for you."

"Great!" shouted Janet and Leon simultaneously.

"But wait," Al said. "The lender won't do that for nothing. It will up the interest rate on your mortgage. Typically it will cost you at least one-eighth of 1 percent, *or more,* to have the lender absorb the costs. If we add that amount of interest to your loan, it will bump up your monthly payments beyond what the lender will allow. The alternative would be to get a smaller mortgage with lower payments and a lower-priced home."

"Bummer," Leon said. Janet nodded agreement.

"Of course," Al added, "There are other alternatives. It might be possible to get a mortgage for up to 103 percent (sometimes more) of the home's value. Here the interest rate wouldn't rise, but the mortgage amount would. However, that also would impact your payments, meaning you'll probably need to get a lower-priced home."

"Can't the seller pay all the buyer's closing costs?" Janet complained.

"Yes, the seller can easily pay all your nonrecurring closing costs (excluding taxes, insurance, interest, and other recurring costs)," Al replied. "You just have to find a seller who's willing to do that."

TRAP

You have to convince a seller to pay the buyer's costs. When the market is slow, some sellers are willing. However, in recent years, with a seller's market (too few properties, too many buyers), few are agreeable.

TIP

The time to negotiate the seller paying the buyer's closing costs is before the deal is made. Lenders usually won't offer a mortgage when the price is negotiated upward. They'll say that the true price was lower and the upward negotiation was to artificially inflate the

financing. If you're going to try and have the seller pay
the buyer's closing costs, the time to do that usually is
when you make the original offer.

Janet shook her head. Convincing a seller to pay the buyer's costs
might be hard to do with houses selling quickly in their area.
"In any event," Al said, "At least you're ready to start looking."

Getting the House

Janet had planned to call Alice, the agent, the next day to ask about
looking at houses. However, Alice called her that night after Al left.
She wanted to know if they had been preapproved. When Janet said
they were, Alice wanted to know how expensive a home they could
afford. Janet said $250,000 and Alice replied, "Let's get looking!"

The next weekend they went house hunting with Alice. It turned
out there were many houses in their area for $250,000 and under.
Leon and Janet looked but couldn't find one that suited them.

The following weekend they looked again, with the same results.
Finally on the third weekend Alice said, "We need to raise our sights
a little. Let's look at some more expensive homes." They began looking at homes up to $275,000.

Almost immediately Leon and Janet found what they considered
to be the perfect place. They only problem with it was that the sellers
were asking $265,000. That was $15,000 more than they could afford.

"Maybe you could borrow some money from relatives," Alice suggested. Leon and Janet shook their heads. That wasn't a possibility.
So, Alice said, "Let's make an offer at $250,000 and see what they do."

Janet called Al and he faxed them a preapproval letter that
showed that they qualified for nothing down at $250,000. She gave
this to Alice along with their signed purchase agreement. Then she
and Leon crossed their fingers and waited.

A few hours later, Alice called back. She said the sellers came
down $5,000 but were adamant about not going lower. She had a
counteroffer for $260,000, but that was the best she could do.

Manipulating the Mortgage

Janet and Leon called Al.

He thought about their predicament, then said they might be
able to get an ARM (adjustable rate mortgage). Some had a fixed

rate built in for five years, then switched to adjustable with adjustments just once a year. If he could find one that offered nothing down, it would lower the interest rate about half a percent. That might increase the mortgage amount by just enough to make the deal. He said he'd call them back.

An hour later Al called to say he was faxing them a new preapproval letter. It said they could get a $260,000 mortgage—and the house!

Janet and Leon whooped for joy. Then, Al's voice came back over the phone. He said they had to understand what they were getting into.

"The new mortgage, like the old one, has 1 point and is amortized (paid back on the basis of 30 years)," Al said. "But where it's different, is that the fixed rate only lasts for five years. After that, it converts to an adjustable rate mortgage. The adjustment periods are once a year, with a maximum adjustment of 2 percent. That means if interest rates rise in the market, your interest rate could rise by as much as 2 percent in year 6. That would mean a 15 percent increase in your monthly payment."

Janet and Leon looked at each other. "But I thought we agreed not to get an ARM," Janet said over the phone.

"This is a kind of hybrid fixed-rate and adjustable rate mortgage," Al said. "I wouldn't recommend it, except that you need more money to get into the home.

"You'll have to keep that five-year time limit in mind. Hopefully, your income will have risen and rates will have remained stable, so you can refinance to a better loan. But if not, you might have to sell—or make higher ARM payments."

TIP

The general rule is that it's a good idea to get a fixed-rate loan when interest rates are low, thereby locking in that low rate. You get an ARM when rates are high and falling, thereby getting an initially lower rate than for a fixed-rate loan and seeing your payments go down. See Chapter 23 for more on ARMs.

"Are there any other alternatives?" Leon asked

"Yes," Al replied. "There are interest-only loans and straight ARMs. But each alternative comes with its own drawbacks. And in your case, there might not be as many alternatives as for others, because you're looking for nothing-down financing. Usually that's only found in fixed-rate loans. The 5/1/ARM I found from a lender is a real exception. I think you should grab it.

TRAP

Interest-only loans often convert to ARMs after a number of years. At that time, however, the principal amount is still the same as it was when the loan was originated, since only interest has been paid. The loan is recast and the result is that the ARM now often has a substantially higher payment.

The Final Mortgage

Leon and Janet signed the counteroffer and the deal was made. Alice pointed out that she had included a finance contingency that said that if for any reason Janet and Leon couldn't get the mortgage they needed, they'd get back their $5,000 deposit.

Janet called Al back the next day and said the deal was done.

There was a pause, then Al said that there might be a problem. Interest rates had taken a bit of a bump up. They might not be able to get the rate he quoted them.

Leon and Janet were astonished. Then Leon said, "But, we based our purchase on the assumption we'd get the loan. What'll we do if we can't?"

"Well," said Al, "assuming that Alice put a finance contingency into the offer, you'll simply lose the deal and get your deposit back. But, before worrying about that, let me call the lender and see what the deal is. I'll call you back shortly."

Janet and Leon waited by the phone. It was three hours before Al called. "Sorry," he said, "but I couldn't get through. There are lots of borrowers looking for loans. I finally talked with the lender. They'll honor our terms—and I locked you in for 30 days."

"Yeah!" Janet said, then explained to Leon what Al had said over the phone. "What does 'lock us in' mean?" Leon asked.

Janet put the question to Al.

"It means that the lender has agreed to hold that rate and terms for no more than 30 days. If the deal hasn't closed and title transferred by then, the rate could go up."

Leon got on the phone. "Do you think we can close that soon?"

Al said he had talked to Alice and she was a determined agent. She felt they could do it.

Leon's mind was working full out. He said, "When you say we're locked in, does that mean we have to go with this lender no matter what? What if rates drop?"

Al paused, then said, "Yes, you're supposed to stay with the lender that gives you a lock. If rates drop, however, I'll ask the lender to lower your rate. If it's a big drop, the lender probably will. If it's a small drop, say a quarter percent or less, the lender won't."

TIP

"Locks" are supposed to lock in both parties, borrower and lender. However, unless the borrowers have paid a fee they don't want to lose for the lock to the lender, there's nothing to prevent them from jumping ship and going to another lender with a lower rate. The only restraining factor is usually time; when working directly with a lender such as a bank, it takes time to get another lender's approval and funding, usually three weeks, at a minimum. However, if you're working with a mortgage broker who's already completed a mortgage package, switching can be done in a matter of a few days.

The Closing

Alice opened escrow, which was like a stakeholder. It was a company that held all documents and money until the deed of trust (the mortgage) to the lender and the deed to the property in favor of Janet and Leon was ready to be recorded. Then it recorded the documents and paid out all funds. Before that could happen, however, during the escrow period the sellers had to prove they had clear title (as evidenced by a policy of title insurance).

It all took about three and a half weeks to accomplish. "Things went well," Al said, intimating that sometimes they didn't go nearly as well.

Finally Janet and Leon got a call from the escrow officer saying their loan documents were ready to sign. When could they come down? They agreed to meet that afternoon.

TRAP

Many things can go wrong. The sellers might have a lien on the property or other title problem that could prevent them from selling. The lender might decide that the borrowers couldn't afford the loan after all (if, for example, they had gone out and made a big purchase, such as a car, which affected their credit score). As the inimitable ball player, Yogi Berra, used to say, "It ain't over 'til it's over."

The escrow officer, Peter, introduced himself and then plopped down on his desk a bunch of papers nearly two inches thick. "I believe these are all ready for you," he said.

"You want us to sign all those?" Leon asked aghast.

"Yes," Peter said, "And I'll need to collect some additional funds."

"You mean for the closing costs." Janet clarified. Peter nodded, then began going through the documents. The first was the note and deed of trust.

TIP

Janet and Leon were in a trust deed state. This is a type of loan instrument that lenders prefer, because it allows for easy nonjudicial foreclosure in the event they defaulted. However, some states still use an older mortgage instrument that requires court approval of foreclosure. See Appendix 2 for more details.

The note was only 3 pages long, but the trust deed was 11 pages of small-type legalese. "Are we supposed to read all this?" Leon asked.

Peter the escrow officer replied, "You can if you want, although I'm really busy today. It's all 'boilerplate.' Most people just sign and then, if they want, read it later at their leisure. It's what the lender requires, so you have to sign it to get the loan."

"But," Janet asked, "shouldn't someone who knows something about these things look at it?"

Peter replied, "You can take it to your attorney if you want. But, just remember we're ready to close and don't have much time."

In the end, they simply signed.

TRAP

You should never sign anything that you haven't read and understand. There could be errors included that are very hard, if not impossible, to correct afterward. And there's often devil to pay in the "boilerplate," as almost anything can be inserted. It's usually better to take the time to read it all and to have your attorney explain to you anything you're not sure about.

Peter then laid out a whole series of documents before Janet and Leon. The first was the Federal Truth-in-Lending Disclosure Statement. It was similar to the one Al had originally given them and detailed the annual percentage rate of the mortgage, all the finance charges over the life of the loan, the total amount financed, the total of all payments, and the total sales price.

"Wow," Janet said. "We'll end up paying something over $250,000 in interest over the life of the mortgage!"

Peter nodded. "That's the price you pay to get a loan."

There was also an occupancy certificate in which they swore they intended to move into the property. They had to sign this form, since it was a condition of getting the particular loan they wanted.

Next came an impound account authorization. It allowed the lender to establish an impound account to pay for their insurance and taxes. "The lender gathers the money from you monthly, then pays it out once or twice a year. It covers hazard insurance and property taxes."

"But," Leon said, "I thought we would pay those ourselves?"

"You could," said Peter, "If you put 20 percent or more down. However, with little or no down, a condition of the loan is that the lender handles this for you."

More documents explained who the lender was and that it might assign the servicing rights of their mortgage.

"What does servicing mean?" Leon asked.

"Mortgage companies earn a fee for collecting the mortgage payment from you. They can sell the rights to collect the payment and earn the fee to other mortgage companies. Or they can sell the mortgage itself, or both. During the life of the loan you may end up making your payment to half a dozen or more different companies as your loan servicing rights are transferred from lender to lender," Peter said.

They then signed a document that stated that they were aware of the appraised value of the house (it had appraised for the full amount) and that they had received a copy of the good faith estimate (a copy of which was included).

"Boy-o-boy," said Janet. "I never realized there was so much paperwork to getting a house!"

"We're almost done," said Peter.

There were more documents to sign, including a fair lending notice that said they had not been discriminated against in getting their financing by the lender and a privacy statement of the lender.

There were also a few strange forms that said that if the lender had made an error on any of the forms, Janet and Leon agreed in advance that the lender could correct it without coming back to them for approval. There was even a letter (left mostly blank) that allowed the lender to check with the Internal Revenue Service to verify their income (Form 4506).

"This is a blank form," Leon said. "I don't want to sign a blank form."

Peter nodded and said that many borrowers completed the dates in the form that allowed the lender to confirm only their income for a specified time, say for a couple of years. Peter filled in some dates, then they signed the form. (See Chapter 24.)

TRAP

The HUD-1 form issued by the escrow agent must disclose all of the costs of the transaction including what the lender is charging. Unfortunately, it only need be given to the borrower one day before closing.

HUD-1 Disclosures

Finally, at the very end, they were presented with what Peter referred to as their HUD-1 disclosure, which he had prepared. It summarized all the expenses and fees they were required to pay. The basic costs that Al had spoken of were already there, the $5,000 in points (2 points) and the $2,000 in escrow and title insurance charges. In addition, there were lender's costs, including the following:

- Document preparation fee from the lender
- Loan origination fee—fee to get the lender's desired *yield* as well as to pay for the mortgage broker

- Loan preparation fee from the lender
- Administrative fee from the lender
- Wire fees from the lender
- Appraisal fee from the lender
- Lender's attorney fee

The closing costs totaled nearly $1,000.

"What are all these?" asked Leon and Janet together.

Peter leaned forward and said, "These last are what are sometimes called 'garbage fees' in the industry. You've got to pay them to get the loan."

TIP

Some lenders, in the minority, do pad their loans with garbage fees. However, if the fee is associated with a service actually performed and is for a reasonable amount, it is not "garbage." It's a true fee that someone has to pay, usually the borrower.

TRAP

In a perfect world, there would be no fees associated with financing a mortgage. When you get a consumer bank loan, normally the bank assumes all charges. It would seem logical that the mortgage lender would also assume all costs and wrap them up into a slightly higher interest rate. However, lenders compete to offer the lowest rates. And the government in some cases determines what can and can't be included in the interest rate. Hence, loan fees, and sometimes when abused, garbage fees.

"But," Janet protested, "we agreed with Al that the lender's own fees wouldn't be more than $2,500 in points plus $1,000. Here they're more than twice that amount."

Peter shook his head. "I wouldn't know about that," he said. "These are the closing documents the lender sent me. You'll have to sign as they are written in order to get the mortgage."

"The devil we do!" shouted Leon. "I want to talk to Al, our mortgage broker."

Peter looked shocked, then said okay. He called Al and said, "They're here, but they're balking at the costs. Do you want to talk to them?" Then he gave the phone to Leon, who read off all the costs on the HUD-1 form.

Al listened, then said, "The lender must have made a mistake. There's not supposed to be more than $1,000 in fees and 1 point." He asked to be put back on the phone to Peter.

They talked a moment, then Peter said to Janet and Leon, "You can either sign these documents as written and Al will try to get the costs refunded to you afterward. Or you can wait until the day after tomorrow, after Al calls the lender and new documents are issued."

Janet and Leon said they'd wait.

TRAP

Waiting may not be an option if you're under the gun to close because of time constraints in the purchase agreement. If, on the other hand, the closing is delayed because the lender made an error in the loan documents, generally the lender will extend a loan lock.

Two days later they were called back to the escrow office. Al was there, and the lender had submitted new costs that Peter had prepared in a new HUD-1 statement. The total loan fees came to exactly $1,000 plus 1 point ($2,500).

Janet and Leon nodded and signed.

The next day the loan funded (the lender sent the funds to the title company), and the day after that the deed of trust and grant deed were recorded with the country recorder. Shortly afterward, Alice presented Leon and Janet with the keys to their new home and they moved in.

The mortgage process detailed here is not unusual. Indeed, it's fairly typical. However, there may be all sorts of other issues that appear. For example, the lender at the last minute may refuse to fund the loan, saying that the borrower's credit score changed. This could happen, for example, if the borrower went out and bought a big-ticket item, such as a car. Or a lien could be suddenly recorded against the seller, holding up title clearance.

The process of getting financing can be easy or arduous, depending on your circumstances and the quality of your mortgage broker and lender. Each new mortgage presents its own separate challenge.

2

Mortgage Selector

I once asked a mortgage broker who had been in the business more than 20 years how many different kinds of mortgages were out there. He answered that he personally handled over 50 types.

When I asked a representative of a mortgage banking trade group, the answer was, "around 800." A rep from Fannie Mae said she'd seen over 2,000.

You get the idea. There are hundreds, perhaps thousands, of different *types* of mortgages out there. Surely with that kind of variety, one or perhaps even many will be perfect for you. But how do you know which one(s)?

It's impossible (and if it were possible, probably fruitless) to examine all the myriad variations that mortgages take today. However, almost all mortgages fall within certain groups: fixed-rate, adjustable rate, interest-only, hybrids, and so forth.

To help you determine both what's out there and what might be most suited to your needs, check into the pages of this chapter. Each page explains a different type of mortgage—what it is, who should get it, its drawbacks, and where to find it. Feel free to make comparisons. (*Note:* A mortgage mentioned here might not be available at the time you are looking. Often, however, you can find one with similar features.)

The remainder of this book (after this chapter) will explain in detail many of these mortgages as well as the tricks of home financing.

Fixed-Rate Mortgage
What Is It?

The interest rate on the mortgage, and hence the monthly payment, is fixed for the life of the loan. No matter if market interest rates go up (or go down), the payment on this loan will not vary. See also Appendix B.

Who Should Get It?

This loan is best for borrowers whose income is relatively stable. If you want to know that your payment isn't going to vary month to month, this mortgage is for you. The best time to get this type of mortgage is when interest rates are low, so you can lock in a low payment for the life of the loan.

Drawbacks

Because you are locked into a fixed rate, if interest rates drop, you could end up paying a higher-than-market rate. The interest rate for this type of loan typically is slightly higher (at any given time) than for an ARM.

Mortgage Sources

Mortgage brokers, banks, savings and loan companies, mortgage bankers, online lenders

Fixed-Rate Mortgage with Balloon

What Is It?

As with a standard fixed-rate mortgage, with a fixed-rate mortgage with balloon the interest rate does not vary. However, unlike with a standard fixed-rate, there is one payment that is significantly larger than all the others, called a "balloon." For example, with a 5/30-year balloon, the payments are calculated as if the loan would pay off in equal payments (amortized) over 30 years. However, at the end of year 5, the remaining balance immediately becomes due and payable. This larger payment is called a balloon because of its increased size. Balloons are often found on second as well as first mortgages. See also Chapter 10.

Who Should Get It?

Because the addition of the balloon shortens the life of the mortgage, lenders may offer a better interest rate than on a full-term 30-year fixed-rate mortgage. This loan is suitable for those who need a lower interest rate and, hence, either a lower payment or larger loan amount (or both).

Drawbacks

The mortgage must be paid off when the balloon comes due. That may necessitate refinancing or selling the property. Short-term balloons can be treacherous and can cause the borrowers to lose the property if they cannot refinance or sell.

Mortgage Sources

Banks, savings and loan companies, mortgage brokers, mortgage bankers, credit unions, online lenders

Adjustable Rate Mortgage (ARM)

What Is It?

The interest rate on this type of mortgage is allowed to fluctuate within very defined limits. For example, the interest rate may move up (or down) after the end of every six months, or one month, or a year as determined by the loan documents. This is called the "adjustment period." Additionally, the amount the interest rate may fluctuate per adjustment may have a maximum, say 1½ percent. This is called the "steps." The interest rate fluctuations are tied to an independent index, with the borrower paying a set amount above that index, the "margin." See more in Chapter 23.

Who Should Get It?

Because the interest rate with ARMs is allowed to fluctuate according to market conditions, there is less risk to lenders. Hence, lenders are often willing to offer a low initial rate (called a "teaser"). If you need lower payments or a higher balance, look here. Also, getting an ARM during periods of high and declining interest rates means that the mortgage payments should eventually go down as interest rates eventually fall.

Drawbacks

After the initial (teaser) low interest rate term expires, the interest rate can often jump to higher-than-market rate (to make up for the low initial rate). Thus, payments can increase dramatically over time. Further, depending on how the index and the margin are set, the long-term interest rate may be higher than market.

Mortgage Sources

Mortgage brokers, banks, savings and loan companies, mortgage bankers, online lenders

Fixed Rate with ARM

What Is It?

This is a fixed-rate mortgage that, after a certain period of time, converts to an ARM. The conversion period may vary and is typically set at three, five, or seven years. For those periods of time, the mortgage is at a fixed rate with fixed payments. At the end of the period, the mortgage converts to an adjustable rate. See also Chapter 10.

Who Should Get It?

Those who want a higher mortgage balance or lower payments, as the result of a lower interest rate, should look at this mortgage. Because the fixed interest rate period is short, there is less risk to lenders from market fluctuations, therefore, they offer a lower initial interest rate. Borrowers must realize, however, that after the fixed-rate period, the payments may jump when the loan converts to an ARM.

Drawbacks

The ARM portion of this mortgage may be ugly. It may be higher than market for most of the life of the loan.

Mortgage Sources

Banks, savings and loan companies, mortgage brokers, mortgage bankers, credit unions, online lenders

Fixed Rate/ARM with One-Year Adjustments

What Is It?

With this type of loan, adjustments can only be made at the end of each year. The loans are typically 3/1, 5/1, and 7/1. The first number is the length of the fixed-rate period. The second number denotes the one-year adjustment period of the ARM. This loan combines a fixed rate and an ARM with set adjustment periods. See also Chapter 23.

Who Should Get It?

Anyone looking for a lower interest rate (lower payments and/or higher mortgage balance) along with more controlled adjustments of the ARM should consider this type of mortgage. Since rates adjust only at one-year increments, the adjustments are less likely to come as a shock to borrowers than ARMs that adjust every six months or even every month.

Drawbacks

The "steps" or amount of adjustment can be high, meaning that although the mortgage adjusts infrequently, those adjustments can be steep.

Mortgage Sources

Banks, savings and loan companies, mortgage brokers, mortgage bankers, credit unions, online lenders

Low-Rate Teaser Adjustable

What Is It?

A low-rate teaser adjustable is usually a straight ARM. The adjustment periods are typically between one month and three years. However, the initial adjustment period interest rate may be very low, as much as half the market rate. See also Chapter 23.

Who Should Get It?

This type of loan is designed for people who must have a very low initial interest rate, often in order to make a purchase, resulting in a lower payment and/or higher mortgage balance for a short time. It's ideal for those who plan to buy and then quickly resell or refinance.

Drawbacks

The low rate lasts only during the teaser period. The shorter the teaser, the quicker payments will shoot up. In some mortgages, after the teaser the interest rate can be increased to compensate for the below-market interest during the teaser period.

Mortgage Sources

Banks, savings and loan companies, mortgage brokers, mortgage bankers, credit unions, online lenders

Capped Interest Rate ARM

What Is It?

With capped interest rate ARMs the interest rate is not allowed to rise beyond a certain amount per adjustment period (capped steps), and beyond a maximum amount for the life of the loan (often twice the current interest rate). Also, the steps (the amount the loan interest rate can rise per adjustment period) are also often capped. See also Chapter 23.

Who Should Get It?

This type of loan is intended for those who want the lower interest rate offered by an ARM yet also want the assurance of limited increases in the interest rate.

Drawbacks

Since the interest rate is capped, when interest rates rise rapidly, the loan may not be able to keep up. The interest lost because of the capping, however, is often charged to the loan in later adjustment periods. Thus, even after market rates stabilize or turn down, the interest rate on this loan may continue upward.

Mortgage Sources

Banks, savings and loan companies, mortgage brokers, mortgage bankers, credit unions, online lenders

Capped Payment ARM

What Is It?

With capped payment ARMs the monthly payment is also capped. No matter how high the interest rate rises, the monthly payment is not allowed to rise beyond a certain point, perhaps 15 percent per adjustment period. An interest rate cap is also included. See also Chapter 23.

Who Should Get It?

This type of loan is intended for those who want the lower initial interest rate offered by an ARM yet also want the stability of limited increases in the monthly payment.

Drawbacks

If the monthly payment is not allowed to rise, and yet the interest charged does rise, a situation may come into existence where the monthly payment is no longer adequate to pay the interest. When this happens the excess interest is added to the principal amount (negative amortization). Thus the amount owed may actually increase, up to a maximum of 125 percent of the original balance. You can end up owing more than you borrowed and paying interest on interest.

Mortgage Sources

Banks, savings and loan companies, mortgage brokers, mortgage bankers, credit unions, online lenders

Adjustable with One-Time Conversion to Fixed

What Is It?

This type of ARM offers the borrower the opportunity to convert to a fixed rate at market once during the loan period. The conversion is typically after year 3 or year 5. See also Chapter 10.

Who Should Get It?

This type of loan is intended for those who want the lower initial interest rate (and correspondingly lower monthly payments and/or higher mortgage balance) of an ARM, yet also want to later be able to get a fixed interest rate and, hence, the fixed mortgage payment.

Drawbacks

Since the date of the one-time conversion is set at the time the mortgage is obtained, it's the luck of the draw as to whether interest rates will be higher or lower (than when the mortgage is obtained) on that date. There is also a slight premium for this mortgage, meaning that the borrower pays extra for the conversion option.

Mortgage Sources

Banks, savings and loan companies, mortgage brokers, mortgage bankers, online mortgage lenders, credit unions

Interest-Only Mortgage
What Is It?

This type of mortgage is a combination fixed-rate and adjustable rate mortgage. The first 5 or 10 years are fixed, after which the loan converts to the ARM. During the fixed-rate period, only the interest is due, not the principal, although usually you may pay an additional amount to principal at any time. Because no payment is made to principal, the payment is less than a traditional loan, where both principal and interested are collected monthly.

Who Should Get It?

If you need a smaller monthly payment to help you qualify or want to save your cash for investment or other purposes, you should consider this type of mortgage.

Drawbacks

No (or little) principal is paid back until the ARM cuts in, then payments increase dramatically. Also, you're not paying down the loan during the fixed-rate period.

Mortgage Sources

Banks, savings and loan companies, mortgage brokers, mortgage bankers, online mortgage lenders

Low-Down/No-Down Conforming Mortgage with PMI

What Is It?

This type of mortgage offers little to no down payment (under 20 percent down to zero down). It usually conforms to the underwriting limits of Fannie Mae or Freddie Mac, the nation's two big secondary lenders. (They "buy" the mortgage from the banks, savings and loan companies, mortgage bankers, and other lenders who issue them.) The loans require that you obtain private mortgage insurance (PMI), which insures the lenders. There is an additional cost for the PMI. (You must also normally intend to move into the property.) See also Chapter 18.

Who Should Get It?

This type of mortgage is intended to help low- to middle-income borrowers purchase homes with little or no cash down. The loan amount, in some cases, can cover many of the closing costs as well. Interest rates are usually the lowest available.

Drawbacks

The PMI adds to the payment and may not be tax deductible (unless the lender self-insures and wraps it into the mortgage interest). It may be difficult getting the PMI removed, even after the home appreciates in value. Check into Chapter 18.

Mortgage Sources

Banks, savings and loan companies, mortgage brokers, mortgage bankers, online mortgage lenders

Low-Down/No-Down Mortgage without PMI

What Is It?

Two loans are combined in this form of mortgage. There is a first mortgage where, since the loan is for no more than 80 percent of value, there is no PMI required. A second mortgage of from 10 to 20 percent is then added to come up with a low-down/no-down combination. Remember, since the amount of the first is 80 percent or less, no PMI is required. See also Chapter 11.

Who Should Get It?

Those who want a lower payment will find this type of loan advantageous. Since there is no PMI, the payment is lower than for loans that require PMI.

Drawbacks

The combined interest rate on the first and second mortgages may be higher than on a single loan, thus nullifying the effects of eliminating PMI. There could be two loan payments to make instead of one.

Mortgage Sources

Banks, savings and loan companies, mortgage brokers, mortgage bankers, online mortgage lenders

No Down Plus Closing
Costs Covered Mortgage

What Is It?

This type of loan funds the full price of the purchase plus an additional 3 or 7 percent, which can then be used to pay for closing costs. It is a conforming loan underwritten by Fannie Mae or Freddie Mac. The borrower's credit score and income are critical to getting it. See also Chapter 11.

Who Should Get It?

This type of loan is good for those who have a regular income but have not saved up money for either a down payment or closing costs.

Drawbacks

These loans usually require a higher interest rate. Also, since they are underwritten by Fannie Mae or Freddie Mac, they cannot exceed the maximum conforming loan limit, currently $359,650.

Mortgage Sources

Banks, savings and loan companies, mortgage brokers, mortgage bankers, online mortgage lenders

125 Percent Mortgage

What Is It?

This is a mortgage package totaling 125 percent of the value of the home. It sometimes consists of a first mortgage, typically for 100 percent, and a second personal loan for the remaining 25 percent. As a result, it can be a combined real estate and a personal loan.

Who Should Get It?

If you need cash and anticipate the value of the property will shoot up, you may want to consider this mortgage. It offers you cash back at the time you obtain the loan.

Drawbacks

It carries a higher interest rate and higher payments than other types of loans. Also, since you owe more than the property is worth, the property will be difficult to resell until values move up. And, if you get into financial trouble, you won't be able to "walk away," since it's usually both a real and a *personal* loan (you personally guarantee repayment).

Mortgage Sources

Mortgage brokers, online mortgage lenders

Low/No-Documentation Mortgage (Liar's Loans)

What Is It?

It can be either a fixed-rate or adjustable rate mortgage or some combination of the two. It does *not* require that you prove your sources of income. You allow the lender to get your FICO credit score. In some, but not all, cases you list only your name and the property address. You may not even need to fill out an application. In the trade, it is spoken of as a "liar's loan" because of the large number of defaults from borrowers who lied on their applications about their income. See also Chapter 8.

Who Should Get It?

If you have undocumented income and cannot qualify for a traditional mortgage, you may want to opt for this type of mortgage. It is usually appealing to those self-employed who may be underreporting income and assets.

Drawbacks

This type of mortgage carries a significantly higher interest rate to offset the additional risk to the lender. If you default on the mortgage, you may later be required to prove that you initially did have sufficient income and resources to get it. There are stiff penalties for lying. See also Chapter 8.

Mortgage Sources

Banks, savings and loan companies, mortgage brokers, mortgage bankers, online mortgage lenders

Jumbo Loan

What Is It?

Any mortgage above the maximum amount for conforming loans (Freddie Mac and Fannie Mae), currently at $359,650, is usually considered a jumbo loan. These are often also called "portfolio loans" because they are made by lenders, such as banks, which then hold the mortgage in their own portfolio instead of selling it on the secondary market. More often, however, they are sold to lenders, such as insurance companies, that specialize in making larger loans. Generally speaking, the minimum down payment is 5 percent up to $650,000 and 10 percent up to $1 million. Larger down payments may be required over $1 million. See also Chapter 13.

Who Should Get It?

Those who live in areas where housing prices exceed the conforming amount, mainly on the coasts and in large cities, should consider this type of loan.

Drawbacks

The interest rate on jumbos can sometimes be higher than for conforming loans. Qualifying can require a high income stream as well as strong credit.

Mortgage Sources

Banks, savings and loan companies, mortgage brokers, mortgage bankers, online mortgage lenders

Bad Credit Mortgage

What Is It?

This is called a "subprime loan," and it is offered to many people who, because of their credit record, cannot qualify for a prime loan (generally considered a conforming loan, see above). Bad credit loans are generally for borrowers who have a credit score below 660. See also Chapter 6.

Who Should Get It?

If you cannot qualify for a prime loan, you may be able to qualify for a subprime program offered by some lenders. Regardless of the term of the loan, you should consider it short term, a mortgage offered to you during a period when you can clean up your credit and qualify for a prime loan.

Drawbacks

Subprime loans usually require a bigger down payment and always carry with them a higher interest rate, sometimes significantly higher (1 to 3 percent or more above market rates), to warrant the risk to lenders. They also may require more points to be paid.

Mortgage Sources

Mortgage brokers, mortgage bankers

Second Mortgage–Home Equity Loan

What Is It?

An additional or second mortgage placed on the property after you already have a first mortgage. (If you have no existing first mortgage, however, a home equity/improvement mortgage can be a first.) Sometimes, a first and second mortgage are combined to avoid payment of PMI (see above) or to get a blended interest rate that's lower than might otherwise be available in a single loan. See also Chapter 15.

Who Should Get It?

If you want to get a lower payment to avoid PMI or a higher interest rate mortgage, a second mortgage could be for you. It's also worth considering if you want to improve your home and keep an existing low interest rate first mortgage. It can offer flexible access to funds (line of credit), and you only pay interest on the money that you actually draw out.

Drawbacks

It ties up the equity in your property, meaning that you'll get less cash out when you sell. Also, you won't have the equity available for other purposes. The second mortgage, because of increased risk, generally requires a higher interest rate.

Mortgage Sources

Banks, savings and loan companies, mortgage brokers, mortgage bankers, online mortgage lenders

Seller's Mortgage

What Is It?

Also sometimes called "creative financing," a seller's mortgage has the seller as the lender. In a transaction, the seller converts some or all of his or her equity into a mortgage (a first, second, or other type mortgage) in favor of the buyer. The term, interest rate, repayment schedule, and amount are determined by the parameters of the transaction. Often the seller will only require a credit report and not a credit score. The decision to make the loan rests upon the judgment of the seller. In a tight "buyer's market," sellers are more predisposed to offer financing. See also Chapter 15.

Who Should Get It?

Buyers and borrowers who cannot qualify for institutional financing, who want unusual repayment terms (for example, no monthly payments until the loan is due), who may be willing to pay a higher interest rate in order to get a lower price (or vice-versa), and who, in general, want to be creative in their financing should consider this type of mortgage.

Drawbacks

Sellers are generally unwilling to offer this financing in a seller's market. They may want an unreasonably high interest rate, or they may balk at a buyer's bad credit.

Mortgage Sources

Sellers only

401(k) Loan

What Is It?

Not strictly a mortgage, this type of loan is money borrowed against a 401(k) retirement plan and then used to help finance the purchase of a home.

Who Should Get It?

Anyone who has a 401(k) plan may qualify for this type of loan. Arrangements must be made through the plan's administrator. Borrowing against the plan means that the funds may not be available at retirement; thus, it is generally inadvisable for borrowers nearing retirement age to use this method.

Drawbacks

The maximum that can be borrowed is 50 percent of account. According to federal rules, the maximum amount that can be borrowed may not exceed $50,000.

Mortgage Sources

401(k) plan administrator

Biweekly Mortgage

What Is It?

Almost any mortgage has regular payments. But, with a biweekly mortgage, the borrower, instead of making payments once a month, makes payments every two weeks. Since there are 52 weeks in a year, that adds up to 13 payments annually. The thirteenth payment goes entirely to principal, which helps pay back the mortgage more quickly. On a 30-year amortized (equal-payments) mortgage, the payback time can be shortened by as much as 25 percent or more. See also Chapter 14.

Who Should Get It?

Those who want to increase the equity in the home and to decrease the term of the loan more rapidly should consider this type of mortgage. Borrowers should have a steady income they can use to make more frequent payments. The payment frequency can be set up by the borrowers themselves, providing the mortgage does not have a prepayment penalty.

Drawbacks

This type of loan is more difficult to repay for those with irregular income, such as entrepreneurs and the self-employed. Some lenders charge an additional fee for setting up a biweekly plan. Many outside companies of dubious financial quality offer to set up the plan for hefty fees.

Mortgage Sources

Borrower, some lenders, outside companies

Bridge Loan

What Is It?

A temporary loan obtained to facilitate the purchase of a new home before the sale of an existing home is a "bridge loan." Usually it is for a short time period (three months to a year) and is for all or some of the amount of the equity in the old home. The bridge loan replaces that equity and is used for the down payment and closing costs on the new home.

Who Should Get It?

This type of loan is designed for home sellers who want to move into a new home before their old home sells. Borrowers must have sufficient equity in the old property to warrant the loan.

Drawbacks

A bridge loan carries a higher interest rate than other types of loans. Also, the borrower now will have double payments, both on the old home and the new one. The short term may be a problem if the old home does not sell in a timely fashion.

Mortgage Sources

Banks, savings and loan companies, mortgage brokers, mortgage bankers, credit cards

Construction Loan

What Is It?

A construction loan is used to facilitate new construction or remodeling. The term of the loan is usually for a year or less. The money is normally paid out in stages as construction is completed. Interest is charged only on the money actually used. This mortgage is often accompanied by a "take-out loan," which is a permanent mortgage intended to replace the construction loan once work is completed. See also Chapter 5.

Who Should Get It?

Anyone who is building or renovating a home and cannot get a conventional mortgage should consider a construction loan. (Lenders will sometimes refuse to issue permanent loans on uncompleted work.)

Drawbacks

A construction loan carries a higher interest rate than many other loans. In order to qualify, you must show either that you're capable of completing the construction or that you're having a licensed contractor doing the work. Bonding might be required of the contractor. This type of loan is typically only short term—one year to 18 months maximum.

Mortgage Sources

Banks

FlexiLoan

What Is It?

This type of mortgage in essence rewrites itself every 30 days. When the borrower receives the monthly payment coupon, he or she can opt to make an interest-only payment, or an ARM payment with negative amortization, or, in some cases, a fixed 20- or 30-year loan payment. The size of the payment will vary, depending on the option selected.

Who Should Get It?

Those who have an irregular income stream and have a need to frequently readjust their monthly payment should consider a FlexiLoan.

Drawbacks

The equity return is often less on this type of loan because the borrower may frequently choose to pay interest only or use the negative amortization ARM. As a result, over time the amount owed may not decrease. (It may actually increase!) Also, the overall interest rate may end up being higher.

Mortgage Sources

Select mortgage brokers and mortgage bankers

No Credit Mortgage

What Is It?

A borrower seeking a no credit mortgage has not established sufficient credit to be able to produce a reliable credit score. The lender has to look to sources other than the credit score to identify the creditworthiness of the borrower. These include records of rent, utility, telephone, and other regular payments as well as check cashing history. See also Chapter 7.

Who Should Get It?

Those who pay mostly by cash and check, who have not established a regular pattern of borrowing, and thus cannot come up with a traditional credit score should consider a no credit mortgage.

Drawbacks

Because of the lack of verifiable credit, the lender may feel it is assuming additional risk and the interest rate on the loan may be higher.

Mortgage Sources

Mortgage bankers

Land Loan

What Is It?

Instead of a home providing collateral for the mortgage, with a land loan land only is the collateral. The land may be developed (utilities and sewer in place) or undeveloped (raw land). See also Chapter 5.

Who Should Get It?

This loan may be available from those who own speculative real estate without improvements on it and wish to sell it to buyers who cannot come up with all cash. Also, the loan may be available as a refinance to get cash out.

Drawbacks

The maximum loan amount is usually not more than 50 percent of the appraised value of the land. Also, a high interest rate may be charged.

Mortgage Sources

Banks

Reverse Equity Mortgage

What Is It?

With a reverse equity mortgage, or REM, the borrower receives a monthly payment instead of making one. Each payment is added to the loan amount and subtracted from the home's equity. Interest is charged only on the amount borrowed and is not collected, usually, until the borrower dies and the home is sold or refinanced. See also Chapter 20.

Who Should Get It?

The mortgage is designed for older borrowers who want to remain in their home yet need additional income to do so. They receive the income in the form of monthly payments essentially taken from the home's equity. Care should be exercised to see that the loan runs for the life of the borrower, lest he or she outlive the property's equity.

Drawbacks

This mortgage requires that the home be paid off or at least have a very large equity. That equity is used up during the life of the loan and, hence, the borrower cannot easily pass the property on as an inheritance. The interest rate can vary, depending on the amount of equity, the age of the borrower, and the monthly payment made to him or her.

Mortgage Sources

FHA, Fannie Mae, and Financial Freedom Plan—See a good banker or mortgage banker.

FHA-Insured Mortgage

What Is It?

The Federal Housing Administration, or FHA, was created during the Great Depression of the 1930s to provide mortgage assistance to borrowers. It offers loans with only 3 percent down. The loans are made by private lenders, but they are insured by the FHA. The insurance premium is roughly 1½ percent of the loan amount and must be paid up front. However, it can be financed as part of the mortgage. There is also a monthly 0.5 percent premium. FHA allows the borrower to finance the closing costs. See also Chapter 16.

Who Should Get It?

An FHA-insured loan is available to those who need low-down-payment financing but who also have excellent credit. It is primarily designed for first-time borrowers, although it is open to anyone. It is aimed at the low- to moderate-income borrower. Types of loans insured include fixed-rate, graduated equity, ARMs, and growing equity mortgages.

Drawbacks

The maximum loan amount is relatively low and varies according to your locale. The current maximum for high-value areas is around $312,000.

Mortgage Sources

FHA insurance through banks, savings and loan companies, mortgage brokers, mortgage bankers

VA (Veterans Administration) Mortgage

What Is It?

This type of mortgage is available to veterans who served during certain periods of eligibility. The VA guarantees a portion of the loan. The maximum loan amount is currently $240,000. There is no down payment required. There is a funding fee for the loan of roughly 2½ to 1¼ percent, depending on the type of service the veteran performed and the down payment, if any. The interest rate may be lower than market in some instances. See also Chapter 16.

Who Should Get It?

The VA mortgage is intended strictly for veterans and is primarily used to purchase low- to moderate-income housing. The veteran must demonstrate the ability to repay the loan, although guidelines are sometimes flexible. It can usually be assumed by a nonveteran, although the originating vet remains responsible.

Drawbacks

The veteran is on the hook to repay the mortgage, sometimes even after selling the property, should a subsequent borrower default. The mortgage amount is low for many areas of the country.

Mortgage Sources

VA guarantee through banks, savings and loan companies, mortgage brokers, mortgage bankers

40-Year Mortgage

What Is It?

It can be any type of mortgage—the difference is that instead of a maximum 30-year amortization period, the amortization is over 40 years.

Who Should Get It?

Those looking for absolutely the lowest payment possible may want to consider this type of mortgage.

Drawbacks

Extending the loan period reduces the payment only slightly, yet it dramatically increases the interest paid over the life of the loan. For example, on a $300,000 mortgage at 6 percent at 30 years, the payment is roughly $1,800. At 40 years at 6¼ percent, it is roughly $1,700, a savings of $100 a month. However, over the life of the loan at 30 years the total interest paid is about $349,000, but on a 40-year loan it is roughly $518,000.

Mortgage Sources

Fannie Mae is offering these on trial basis. Check to find the lenders at www.fanniemae.com or 800-732-6643.

3

Critical Questions to Ask When Getting a Mortgage

Over 10 million people this year will seek new mortgages either to finance the purchase of a new home or to refinance their old home. If you've picked up this book, chances you are one of them.

Yet, the process of getting a mortgage remains mysterious and arcane for most. To be sure, you want to pay the lowest interest rate and get the lowest monthly payments. And you don't want to get caught paying for "garbage fees," unwarranted charges by the lender. Qualifying for the mortgage is another big issue for many borrowers.

Indeed, while mortgage money is gushing out from lenders these days, finding just the right mortgage can be a daunting task. This is especially the case if it's your first home or if you haven't been through the real estate financing process in the past few years.

To help you get started, in this chapter we're going to address some of the most frequently asked questions about mortgages. Along the way we'll learn the ABCs of real estate finance.

Can I Buy for Nothing Down?

Certainly. There are many programs for those in the moderate- to low-income categories. There are also ways for investors to purchase with no money down. Today, loans for 97 to 107 percent of the value of the property are common.

TRAP

Generally speaking, unless the market is skyrocketing and you can quickly resell for a profit, it's often a poor idea for *investors* to purchase with nothing down. The reason is that the high monthly payments often translate into a big "negative cash flow," meaning you must take money out of your pocket each month to support the property. Don't be taken in by the increasing numbers of gurus who promote nothing-down investing through testimonials on tapes and seminars. Ask yourself, if it were such a panacea, why would anyone bother to sell books, tapes, and seminars on the subject? Why wouldn't they simply keep it a secret, do it themselves, and make their fortune in real estate instead of the talk circuit?

TIP

The down payment is *not* the only consideration when mortgage hunting. The monthly payment is just as, if not more, important.

How Do I Determine the Mortgage Payment?

Any loan officer, online mortgage wizard, or amortization table can quickly tell you what your mortgage payment will be. (Check into Appendix A in the back of this book.) It's simply a mathematical function of the interest rate, the term (how long you're borrowing), and the amount you borrow.

The real question is, how can you get your mortgage payments down? This is the real reason that most people shop interest rates. The rate moves up and down daily, usually in small increments. For most people those fluctuations are of little interest. (Do you *really* care if its 6¼ or 6½ percent?). It begins to matter, however, when it gets personal. On a $200,000, 30-year mortgage a quarter percent difference is about $30 a month, and for many that's an important consideration month in and month out.

TIP

Don't just think interest rates. You can also lower your payments by getting a longer term, putting more money down, or buying a less expensive property.

Should I Put More Money Down, If I Can?

The *investment* way of thinking is to put as little down as possible. That way you maximize your leverage. If you put 5 percent down and your property goes up 5 percent in value, you've made 100 percent on your investment. If you put 50 percent down and the property goes up the same 5 percent in value, you made only 10 percent. Thus, the argument goes, you maximize your profit potential by putting down as little as possible.

On the other hand, most people are buying shelter ahead of investment. And the more you put down, the lower your payment, and the lower the payment, the more secure most people feel. A paid-off house can be one of the most secure feelings in the world. This speaks well for putting in a bigger down payment, if you can.

Besides, if you have the money, what are you going to do with it if you don't put it into a house? As of this writing, interest rates are historically low. If you're doing well to get a few percent invested in bonds or elsewhere on your money, it may make more sense to stick it into the home where it might earn far more over time.

What Are Points?

Each point represents 1 percent of a mortgage. Three points for a $100,000 mortgage, therefore, is $3,000. If the mortgage is $150,000 and there are 2 points, it comes to $3,000.

Points are charged by a lender to increase the "yield," or the true return on money loaned. It is usually possible to reduce the number of points required to get a mortgage by paying a slightly higher interest rate.

Where Do I Get a Mortgage?

There are many sources of mortgage loan money, including mortgage brokers (listed as such in the yellow pages of your phone book), banks, savings and loan institutions, credit unions, and direct and indirect lenders on the Internet.

The truth of the matter, however, is that while a great many people are eager to lend you money, what you want is someone who is willing to lend at the lowest interest rate and for the fewest costs. That's where shopping around pays off.

How Long Does It Take to Get a Mortgage?

The time frame varies, depending on whether or not you have any credit problems. Today you can usually get an answer and preapproval within a few days, because underwriting is done electronically.

The time to fund the mortgage (when the lender actually sends the money to the escrow company) also can take a varied amount of time but is usually around a minimum of three weeks. A second credit check is done, and if your credit has changed, or something was missed initially, there can be a holdup. Also, if the lender doesn't happen to have funds immediately available, it could add a few more days as well.

What Is Preapproval and Should I Get It?

This is a letter stating that a lender is willing to give you for a mortgage, up to a certain amount. It is often given before you locate a property and can be used to convince a seller to sell to you.

TRAP

There's an important difference between getting a solid letter of commitment from a lender and simply being qualified. Anyone can qualify you for a mortgage—the real estate agent, the mortgage broker, even the folks at your local gas station. Usually it's nothing more than asking a few questions about your income and expenses to see how big a mortgage you are likely to get. You can do it yourself with the amortization table in Appendix A of this book. However, getting qualified really means nothing without the backing of a lender. It's having the lender commit, saying that you will get a mortgage for a certain amount at a certain interest rate ("you're preapproved") and term that carries water.

How Do I Lock in a Low Interest Rate?

Most lenders will hold, or "lock in," an interest rate for a period of time, typically around 30 to 45 days. This means that if interest rates go up, you get to pay the old rate that was in effect when you locked in your loan. But, you must ask for the lock-in feature—many lenders won't volunteer it and some charge extra for it.

The drawback is that in many cases, if you lock in a rate and rates go down, you're committed to the older, higher rate. This may be only a minor problem, however, because if the lender refuses to give you the new, lower interest rate, you can always go to another lender, if you have time (unless you've paid a fee for the lock-in, which you would then lose). Some lenders will now give you the benefit of a lower rate without any hassle. If the rates go up, you're locked in; if they go down, you get the lower rate, or at least a lower rate than the lock-in.

TIP

It's hard to switch lenders late in the game—you lose time, and time lost can mean a deal lost.

TRAP

Beware of paying a big fee for a lock-in. During times when the rates are rising and lots of people are refinancing as well as buying, some lenders will charge up front for the lock-in. If it's a minimal fee, say $35, you may want to pay for it. But if it's higher, consider carefully. It may be cheaper to reapply later on when rates may go down. (Time, of course, is a consideration, but given the speed with which it is possible to process some loans today, it's not as big a concern as in the past.)

How Much Will My Mortgage Fees Cost?

The actual amount of your mortgage fees are determined by your lender. They will vary, sometimes greatly, depending upon the lender you use. The federal government under the Real Estate Settlement Procedures Act (RESPA) requires the lender to give you a "good faith estimate" of these charges when you apply. But, the government does not currently regulate which charges are reasonable and which are excessive.

Watch out for "garbage fees." These are unwarranted charges that lenders slap on, which can sometimes amount to hundreds of dollars.

Can I Get a Bigger Mortgage Than My Lender Offers?

Maybe, but you'll need to shop around.

The amount you can borrow is determined by your financial profile and includes the following factors:

- You (and your spouse's) income
- Your credit history (how much have you borrowed, how promptly you have repaid it)
- The amount of your down payment
- Your financial resources (net worth)
- How much you already owe to others and other factors

Some lenders are more conservative than others. Some lenders "sell" your mortgage to quasi-government organizations such as Fannie Mae and Freddie Mac (discussed in Chapter 5), and they have very strict guidelines. Other lenders hold your mortgage themselves, and their guidelines may be more liberal. Some lenders don't care at all about your financial profile, but they just lend based on the property's value.

Also, you may be able to arrange a second or even a third mortgage from a lender in addition to the first mortgage. Or the seller may be willing and able to carry back a loan from you.

All of these and other strategies are discussed in various chapters in this book.

Is There Any Advantage in Getting a Shorter-Term Mortgage?

Yes, there are two big advantages and one big disadvantage.

The first advantage is that you can usually get a lower interest rate. Cut the mortgage term from 30 to 15 years and you can probably save a quarter to a half a percent or more in the annual interest. Take it down to seven or even three years and you may be able to save more. The shorter the term of the loan, the lower the interest rate and, consequently, the lower the monthly payment.

The second advantage is that you save enormously on the total amount of interest borrowed. A 15-year loan saves more than half the interest paid over the course of a 30-year loan. It's simply that you're paying interest for fewer years.

The big drawback is that very often the shorter-term mortgage carries a bigger monthly payment. For example, if you borrow $100,000 at 8 percent for 30 years, your monthly payment will be $734. Drop that same loan to 15 years and your monthly payments jumps up to $956, an increase of $222, or 23 percent.

TIP

Many modern loans offer a 30-year payment plan, but with a 3-, 5-, 7-, or 10-year balloon. For example, a common loan today is the 7/30. It is all due and payable within 7 years, although your payback schedule is based on 30 years. As a result, you get the advantage of a lower interest rate (because it's due in 7) and a lower monthly payment (based on 30 years). The drawback is that at year 7, your mortgage isn't fully paid off and you owe a substantial amount, the "balloon" payment.

How Is a Mortgage Different from a Car Loan?

When you borrow on a car it's essentially a "chattel" or personal property loan. You can take the car with you (hide it or move it out of state) and that increases the risk to the lender. Hence, car loans generally are for a higher interest rate (unless the manufacturer is helping with the costs). Also, if you fail to make payments, not only can the car be repossessed but you can still be held liable for repayment of the loan—it's personal property.

When you borrow on a home, it's a real property loan, which is called a "mortgage" or, in a different form, a "trust deed." The property is the primary security, and since you cannot move it, and it is largely protected from destruction by fire and other insurance, the risk and, accordingly, the interest rate tend to be lower.

Also, if you fail to make payments, while the property may be foreclosed (taken back by the lender), in most cases (but not all) you will not be held responsible if the sale of the property does not yield enough money to pay off the mortgage plus costs.

TIP

Some states have "purchase money laws," which give you added protection. If part of the purchase price of a home is a mortgage, the lender may not be able to come back at you personally if the house is sold at foreclosure and does not bring enough money to pay back the loan. You can, essentially, walk away from such a house (although this could have a disastrous effect on your credit).

How Much Information about Myself Must I Tell the Lender?

You will probably have to tell more than you will feel comfortable with. The lender will want to know everything about your finances. This includes:

- Your income from *all* sources
- Your reserves, including all bank and brokerage accounts

- Any problems you may have had with foreclosures, bankruptcies, repossessions, and late payments
- How long you've been employed (two years' worth of 1040 tax statements are needed, if you're self-employed)
- How you much you currently pay in rent or mortgage payments
- What your credit card debt is and how much you pay monthly
- Whether you pay or receive alimony or child support
- All other expenses, including utilities and even phone
- If you are in any stage of a divorce

In short, the lender wants to know you as well as you know yourself in order to make a risk determination. The lender will conduct a three-bureau credit report (from the three nationwide credit reporting agencies; see Chapter 7), which paints a complete financial picture.

TRAP

Remember, what you don't tell the lender it may find out through credit checks. It's better to be up front with an explanation rather than to have an unhappy surprise later on.

What Are the Steps Involved in Getting a Mortgage?

There are seven steps to getting a mortgage. These will be discussed throughout this book, but they are presented here so you can get a better picture of the process involved.

Seven Steps in the Mortgage Process

1. *Get a preapproval letter from a lender* (including an initial credit check and score).
2. *Make a home purchase and decide which lender offers the best financing at the time.*
3. *Apply for the mortgage.*

4. *Supply all necessary documentation* (such as bank records, 1099 or W-2 forms, and paycheck stubs).

5. *Get a property appraisal.*

6. *Wait for the underwriter's approval.* (If there is an underwriting problem, you may need to increase the down payment or lower the borrowed amount.)

7. *Wait until the lender funds the money* (including a final credit check), then close the deal.

What's the First Thing I Should Do to Get Started?

Get preapproved.

You can make a decision later on the type of mortgage you want. You can even decide later on the house you want to buy. But, in order to be a competitive buyer in today's marketplace, you need to get a preapproval letter of commitment from a lender. It will help you determine how big a mortgage, and consequently how pricey a house, you can afford. And, it will make you more acceptable to a seller and therefore help you negotiate a better price and terms.

4

How Do I Get Preapproved?

Preapproval has become a critical step in the purchase of real estate. Today, more buyers than ever use it. It's helpful to determine how big a mortgage and how high a payment you can afford. It's also a useful negotiating tool with sellers.

What we're talking about is a letter that you obtain from a lender telling whoever wants to know (usually meaning the sellers), that you're preapproved to get a loan up to a certain amount at a certain interest rate and term. In a way it's like a blank check—all you have to do is fill in the seller's name and the money gets funded.

No, of course it's not that easy. The deal still has to go through the sales process, and if your job or financial situation changes, you still might not get the mortgage. But it's a solid indication of your creditworthiness.

Does Preapproval Really Help with the Purchase?

A friend recently sold a property to buyers who presented her with a preapproval letter. I think her reactions to it can be enlightening.

The home was in the San Fernando Valley area of Los Angeles at a time when the market was very hot. The seller had only placed

67

the home on the market two weeks earlier when she received calls from three brokers, all of whom wanted to present offers. She told them to bring them all in. (Sellers should receive all offers as they are presented, not simply consider them one at a time in turn.)

All the offers were for around the asking price, $5,000 separating the highest from the lowest. Offer A wanted the seller to carry back a second mortgage to help the buyer make the purchase. Offer B offered 10 percent down to a new mortgage. Offer C likewise offered 10 percent down to a new mortgage but also included a preapproval letter. Offer C was for $1,000 less than offer B. Offer A was for the most amount of money.

A = Highest offer, carry back second

B = Second-highest offer, 10 percent down to new mortgage

C = Third-highest offer, 10 percent down to a new mortgage *with* a preapproval letter

Which would you accept? The seller in our example didn't want to carry back any paper (second mortgage), so even though Offer A was the highest-priced offer, she rejected it. (Indeed, the reason the offer was higher was probably because it was weaker—not all cash to the seller.)

The choice, therefore, was between B and C. Offer B was $1,000 higher than C, but C had the preapproval letter.

The seller countered back on C (the one with the preapproval letter), asking for a higher price. And C agreed, and the deal was made.

What made the difference? The preapproval letter. It assured her that if she signed the deal with C, those buyers had an excellent chance of getting a mortgage and the deal could be quickly concluded. The preapproval letter was the determining factor, the critical element.

While the circumstances may be different in homes on which you make offers, don't think the importance of the preapproval letter is exaggerated. It makes sellers sit up and pay attention. And it can get you a deal, sometimes a better deal, than a competing buyer who doesn't have such a letter or has a letter that's of lesser quality. (We'll discuss this subject shortly.) In a slower market than in our example, it can even save you money on the price. (The seller might accept a lower offer, if it's the only offer, with a preapproval letter.)

What Should Go into the Preapproval Letter?

It's important to understand that what we're talking about here is an informal document. There is no set "government form." In a way it's like a letter of credit that a bank might issue. Each bank's letter will look somewhat different from the others, although certain important elements will be common to all.

TRAP

Today in real estate there are a whole bunch of different letters that are called "qualifying letters." These range from a true lender's commitment to a letter from a broker stating an opinion regarding the borrower's ability to get financing. Savvy sellers, and their agents, read the fine print in these documents to determine what they actually do and don't say.

The key to the preapproval letter is the level of commitment that a lender gives. Is the lender going out on a limb by stating that you definitely can get a mortgage? Or is the lender hedging its bets with all sorts of conditions? Here are some statements that might go into a letter and what they mean:

Firm commitment. The lender commits to offer a mortgage to the buyer (up to a maximum amount and interest rate) subject only to the buyer's financial condition not changing prior to close of escrow (and, of course, the property appraising out). This means that the buyer has fully qualified with the lender that will make the loan. The only things that could go wrong would be something such as the buyer losing his or her job.

Limited commitment. The lender commits to offer a mortgage to the buyer, up to a maximum amount and terms, subject to the buyer's completing any or all of the following:

- *Application.* Sometimes a mortgage broker will simply take your application over the phone, will check nothing out, will have you sign nothing, and will then issue a qualifying letter. This letter will state that you are qualified, but it usually has a clause in it that says your qualification is "subject to verification of credit, bank statements, employment and completing an application." In other words, it's based on nothing more than your own verbal comments.

- *Credit check.* The buyer has presumably completed an application and, based on the statements made, the lender has offered the letter. But, because the lender has not checked the buyer's credit, the lender is holding back a firm commitment. The lender is saying, essentially, "Yes we'll make the loan *if* the buyer's credit proves to be as good as he or she says it is." Again, this isn't much to go on. An old rule in this business is that everyone's credit is perfect until the credit report comes in.

- *Documentation.* The buyer has presumably completed both an application and a credit check. What's missing are documents such as proof of employment; proof of resources, including the cash for the down payment; and other sources of income (such as alimony). If only this documentation is missing, it's a pretty good letter. With documentation, the lender may be willing to give a firm commitment.

TIP

In all of these letters of commitment, there is also a statement saying that the property must appraise high enough to qualify for the mortgage. If the seller's property doesn't appraise out, obviously there will be no loan.

Who Should Issue the Commitment Preapproval Letter?

Ideally, the commitment preapproval letter should come directly from the lender. If you're working with a bank, savings and loan, or credit union, that party is the one to give it. (It may be hard, however, to get a firm commitment letter from some of these institutions.)

Nevertheless, these days chances are you may not be working directly with the lender. Instead, you'll be working with a mortgage broker, a third party that represents a great many lenders. Thus, the mortgage broker may issue the letter.

TIP

It's a good idea to have the preapproval letter made out just before you make an offer and for just enough money to make the deal. (The lender/mortgage broker can fax it to your agent.) If the seller thinks you can qualify for a bigger mortgage than you offer, it may encourage that seller to counter your offer for more money. Keep the sellers guessing about how big a mortgage you can actually get.

How Much Does the Preapproval Letter Cost?

If you have the lender send your application through underwriting at Fannie Mae or Freddie Mac, there is a fee to the lender for that. Usually, however, the lender doesn't charge you, the borrower, for this. It's done as a service in the hopes that you will then use that lender when you actually take out the mortgage. However, real estate is an industry where it seems everyone is constantly adding fees. It wouldn't surprise me in the least to very soon have lenders charging a small amount (probably in the range of $100) for such letters.

There are, however, other incidental fees that you may be charged. There is a credit check fee to the lender, who can be expected to pass that on to you. Sometimes a lender will waive this fee if you actually get the mortgage through him.

TIP

A three-bureau credit check goes to the three national credit checking agencies: Experian, Equifax, and TransUnion. The three-bureau check looks up your credit history in each and produces a combined report. It is useful to lenders, because it reveals credit information anywhere in the country. (See Chapter 7.)

TRAP

There's usually a time limit on the preapproval letter, even if it doesn't say so. Typically such letters are good for around 30 to 90 days. After that, it might be necessary to go through the process again to verify that your financial status hasn't changed.

5

Where Do I Get a New Mortgage?

When you are buying a home, just as when you are refinancing, you will quickly discover that it's up to you to locate financing. In some cases the real estate agent may direct you to a mortgage broker who may be located in the office. In other cases you may be given a list of lenders and told to contact one or more. Or you can always go to the phone book and look under "mortgages."

In all cases, even when you are led to a person who handles mortgages, it is up to you to get the best mortgage for your needs. Just remember that regardless of who offers you the mortgage, there are only five basic sources of funds, as described in the list that follows. What you are after is the best deal for you, not the necessarily the most conveniently located source.

TRAP

Don't be swayed by the fact that your agent recommends one lender over another. What you are after is the least expensive loan you can get. Money is money. You owe it to yourself to investigate several lenders to be sure you're getting the best deal available.

When you apply for a mortgage on a home today, there are essentially five sources. These include:

1. Commercial and savings banks, and savings and loan institutions
2. Credit unions
3. Mortgage bankers
4. Mortgage brokers
5. Online lenders

These are called "retail sources" because they deal directly with the consumer, you.

Should I Try a Bank or an S&L?

Historically, the largest lenders on residential real estate were the savings and loan associations (S&Ls). Today, most go by a different name: a savings bank. With the collapse of the Federal Savings and Loan Insurance Corporation (FSLIC) in the late 1980s, many S&Ls converted to banks and joined the Federal Deposit Insurance Corporation (FDIC). Thus, in your town, yesterday's S&L may be today's savings bank. The change is more than in name only. The way the institution handles funds and makes loans may also be slightly different.

Both commercial banks (which tend to specialize in business loans) and savings banks (which specialize in real estate loans), as well as those remaining S&Ls, offer a wide variety of mortgages, including both fixed-rate and variable-rate loans.

TIP

If you are looking for an FHA-insured or VA-guaranteed home mortgage, a bank is still a good source. Also, if you're looking for a construction loan, because it is of a short duration, a bank will usually be in a position to offer you better terms than most other lenders.

What Is a Mortgage Banker?

Although well known in the lending industry, mortgage bankers are still not so well known among consumers. A mortgage banker is like a bank that doesn't offer commercial services such as checking or savings accounts. It simply offers mortgages.

The way it works is that the mortgage banker funds your loan with its own money. Then it "sells" your mortgage to a secondary lender such as Fannie Mae or Freddie Mac. This "sale" gives the mortgage banker back most of the money it loaned to you. The mortgage banker, however, usually still has a small interest in the mortgage and continues to receive a small percentage of the interest you pay plus (often) a fee for collecting the payments.

What Is a Mortgage Broker?

Mortgage brokers are the most popular sources of mortgages today. They function as mortgage "retailers." In lending, as elsewhere, there is wholesale and then there is retail. The mortgage broker is a retailer—he or she is retailing a loan to the consumer, you.

Mortgage brokers usually represent many lenders. They are the salespeople for banks, savings banks, mortgage bankers, insurance companies, and others who want to offer mortgages but who don't want to deal directly with the public.

A mortgage broker is often licensed by the state to deal with mortgages. (Some states, such as California, do not have a separate mortgage broker's license, but instead require a real estate license.) Sometimes they are individuals who came out of banking. Other times they are former real estate agents whose strong suit was finance.

They arrange with lenders to market their product (mortgages) to the consumer (you) for a fee. (It can be a flat fee, say $1,500, or a percentage of the mortgage, such as 1 or 1½ percent.) When you deal with a mortgage broker, that person is getting a fee for finding and servicing you, including taking the application, finding and assembling all the documentation, and working out any problems.

TIP

Mortgage brokers normally don't get a fee from the lender unless you actually get the mortgage. Therefore, they are definitely on your side and will often stretch to help you get the loan wherever possible.

TRAP

Mortgage brokers sometimes try to charge you fees in addition to those they receive from the lender. This can be in the form of extra points or extra direct costs. I wouldn't pay these. Find out up front what the charges for working with a mortgage broker will be. If he or she is adding on extra costs, find another broker who isn't.

Note: Today mortgage brokers can be the salespeople not only for an insurance company in a distant state but also for the bank across the street. They often represent as many as 100 different lenders and usually offer you the biggest selection when mortgage hunting.

TIP

You might be tempted to go to the bank across the street and offer to borrow from them directly, *if* they will save you the fee they offer the retailer, the mortgage broker. Usually attempts to circumvent the mortgage broker's fees are unsuccessful. You want only one loan; the mortgage broker brings in hundreds. No lender is going to cut its own throat by undercutting its retailers. (A possible exception is the case of online lenders.) You'll find that the charges are typically the same whether you deal directly with the lender (when you can) or with a mortgage broker.

TRAP

Almost any agent who has a real estate license can also get a mortgage broker's license. That entitles the agent to collect a fee for getting a mortgage for you. However, not all mortgage brokers are able to arrange loans at retail. In fact, some agents who call themselves mortgage brokers actually arrange mortgages at *above* retail. In other words, they do for you what you can do for yourself, and then they charge you a fee for it. For example, they may arrange a mortgage for you through a bank and then charge you 1 point above what the lender charges for their services. If you had gone to the lender directly or to a true retailer, it wouldn't have cost you the extra 1 point. Beware of these self-styled mortgage brokers. You don't need them. Shop around to find out the true costs.

Credit Unions

A credit union is a lender that is not subject to the same kinds of taxes and regulations as a bank and that caters to a special group. Hence, it can afford to offer mortgages at slightly lower costs to you.

There are more than 15,000 credit unions nationwide. In the past, many of them dealt primarily in short-term consumer and auto loans. However, during the 1980s the major auto manufacturers began offering their own financing, and this development put a dent into the credit unions' ability to find borrowers. As a result, they turned increasingly to mortgages.

As credit unions expanded their offerings and attracted more people, the banks protested. The courts responded by indicating that credit unions must make loans only to special groups whom they represent, not to the general public.

Today, if you are in the group they service, many credit unions can offer you a wide variety of mortgages. The big catch, of course, is that you must be a member of the credit union in order to borrow from it.

TIP

If you belong to a credit union, check out the terms it is offering on mortgages. When compared with other lenders, it may come out looking more favorable. Remember, money is money, and if the credit union gives you a better deal, why not take it?

Online Lenders

An increasingly large segment of the mortgage lending industry is handled by online lenders. These are usually mortgage brokers who operate over the Internet. They may operate in all 50 states, or they may be licensed in only a particular state.

Online mortgage brokering has come of age. The application is taken online. The credit check is performed electronically. In some cases, the appraisal can be handled electronically, although in most cases a physical inspection is required.

As a borrower, the only time you may actually see a representative of the lender is when you show up at escrow to sign your documents.

Online lenders offer competitive rates. Their big advantage is that you can do the shopping yourself at your leisure from your home.

What Are Secondary Lenders?

It's not necessary to know what secondary lenders are in order to get a good consumer mortgage. But, if you do know, it could help you to understand the process and, in so doing, locate the best lender for you.

Secondary lenders include:

- Quasi-government organizations such as Fannie Mae and Freddie Mac
- Insurance companies
- Out-of-state banks
- Other large companies involved in loaning mortgage money

These institutions almost never deal directly with you, the consumer. Rather, they go through retailers such as mortgage bankers or mortgage brokers (banks can act as retailers for them as well).

When you apply for a mortgage through a retailer, the application you fill out is typically forwarded to a secondary lender for underwriting approval. If it is approved, you get your loan. If it isn't, you don't. The secondary lenders, ultimately, are the ones who make most mortgage loans in America.

What Is the Difference between a "Conforming Loan" and a "Portfolio Loan"?

It is also helpful to know the difference between a "conforming loan" and a "portfolio loan." A conforming loan is one that meets the underwriting limits of Fannie Mae or Freddie Mac, the two big quasi-government secondary lenders. Generally, that means it's within their guidelines, including a maximum amount, currently $359,650. Any loan for more than this amount is called "nonconforming." Any loan not underwritten by Fannie Mae or Freddie Mac is called "nonconforming."

What Is a "Portfolio Loan"?

A portfolio loan is a mortgage that a lender does not sell on the secondary market but instead holds in its own portfolio. A bank may offer you a loan and then fund the money out of its own reserves and collect the interest. Many jumbos (loans over the maximum) are portfolio loans.

TRAP

Technically speaking, only those mortgages actually sold to Freddie Mac and Fannie Mae are conforming. Yet, some lenders refer to their own portfolio loans for less than $359,650 (currently the maximum) as conforming. It's just a matter of linguistics.

How Do I Get a Mortgage, Fast?

Sometimes our concern is with getting the loan promptly so that a deal can go through (or because we need the money from a refinance). Speed is the critical factor.

If you are a prime borrower (that is, have good credit, as described in Chapter 6), you may indeed be able to get a mortgage very fast. In fact, today's computerized mortgage underwriting may allow you to be approved in less than an hour and to have the mortgage funded in less than three weeks! The key is that you must be a strong borrower. You must qualify for an A or at the minimum A– mortgage (that is, have a credit score generally in the 680 or higher range; see Chapter 6).

These fast mortgages are basically underwritten through two electronic programs—Loan Prospector of Freddie Mac and Desktop Underwriter of Fannie Mae. If you meet their profile requirements, you may be able to get the mortgage almost immediately.

Call your nearest mortgage brokers. Ask them if they handle "automated mortgage underwriting." If they don't know what you're talking about or if they say they handle everything but can't be specific about getting a loan approved by an underwriter within an hour, call elsewhere.

TIP

Also try calling a mortgage banker (look in the yellow pages) who deals directly with consumers. Many are now electronically connected and able to handle automated underwriting.

When you find a mortgage broker who handles automated underwriting, you'll be asked to come up with a minimum of documentation.

A normal loan often requires that you get a written statement from your employer verifying your employment and telling the lender that you're likely to continue to be employed. You'll also need a statement from your bank verifying that you have the money for the down payment and closing costs on deposit.

For the fast mortgage, however, all you typically need is a paycheck stub, a savings book that shows amounts on deposit, and your last W-2 form. (You also may be asked to bring down a few other documents that you're likely to have readily available, such as a utility bill or driver's license.) You'll fill out a standardized application. It has about 60 questions that ask everything you can imagine about your financial condition. You will also be asked to come up with around $35 for a credit report and will have to give permission for the lender to check your credit and other financials.

After the application is filled out and you sign it, if you're at a mortgage broker's office, the broker will enter the information into a computer screen. (This is what takes most of the time!)

Once the information is entered, the broker will send it electronically to a lender (for example, a bank or mortgage banker) for qualifying. The lender will scan the form and make a quick judgment as to whether or not you will qualify as a prime borrower. The lender will also look for any questions not answered or information left off and may call the mortgage broker and ask for these.

The lender takes care with this step, because the next one costs money, and usually the lender isn't willing to pop for the cost unless it feels you'll survive the scrutiny.

If the lender feels you'll qualify and the form is properly filled out, it then sends it electronically to either of the two big underwriters in New York (Fannie Mae or Freddie Mac). They receive it in their computers and the computers automatically scan the application and determine whether or not you meet the profile for which they are looking.

If you meet the profile, the computers then access the big credit reporting companies and draw out your credit report. (Remember, you paid for this up front.) It will then get a credit score, typically from FICO (Fair Isaac Corporation, see Chapter 7), and will either pass you, pass you conditionally provided you meet certain criteria, or suggest that perhaps you might not be an appropriate candidate for a conforming loan.

In some cases, the computer can also access a data bank that contains appraisals for some properties. This primarily applies to properties in the East and Midwest, which tend to remain stable in price for long periods of time and for which comparable sales are readily available. If accessibility to such a data bank is possible, the underwriter can approve the property at roughly the same time it approves you!

TIP

Computerized appraisal is still in its infancy. As of this writing, relatively few properties are in the data bank. Chances are you'll have to get a real-life appraiser out there to check out the home you want to buy or refinance.

If you're a "go," the computer can also open escrow, order a title search and title insurance, and also contact an appraisal company and schedule an appraisal for you! In point of fact, however, usually this is done by the primary lender and the mortgage broker.

Usually, within minutes you have your answer. If it's positive, your mortgage is on the way. A few lenders can fund these automated mortgages within as few as three days, although most take several weeks.

TRAP

If you're not a prime borrower, you won't be able to take advantage of this automated electronic system. In that case, you'll have to do it the old-fashioned way, that is, wait for loan approval from a board of directors. This process typically takes four to five weeks or more. As of this writing, most subprime lenders simply haven't adopted the electronic automated lending described here for Fannie Mae and Freddie Mac.

6

Loans for Prime and Subprime Borrowers

(How Lenders View Borrowers)

Whenever I'm asked about how big a mortgage a person can get, I'm reminded of that old saw about two speculators in New York City who wanted to buy a $20 million office building. After a meeting with the lender, one returned to the other and said, "There's good news and there's bad news."

"What's the good news?" asked the partner.

"They've agreed to loan us the mortgage money."

"Good," said his friend, "Then what could be the bad news?"

"They're requiring that we put $500 down."

The simple truth is that if you want a mortgage, you have to meet the lender's requirements no matter how illogical they may seem. Sometimes the requirements are easy. Other times they are very difficult to meet.

In this chapter we are going to begin by looking at prime A loans. (Later on we'll look at the subprime market.) These are the most popular mortgages because they offer the lowest interest rates and costs. They are also sometimes called "conforming loans" because they conform to the underwriting limits of Fannie Mae and Freddie Mac, the two large quasi-government secondary lenders that "buy" the mortgages from the lenders who loan the money to you.

These loans have a maximum amount that changes as housing prices go up. (Currently the maximum is $359,650.) They also require that you have sterling credit.

If you want to see whether you're likely to qualify for one of these mortgages, check into the short quiz at the end of this chapter.

TIP

Most prime mortgages are available only if you intend to occupy the property.

How Do Lenders Evaluate You?

How do lenders of prime loans discriminate between those who get mortgages and those who don't? How does a lender determine how big a mortgage you can get? How little you must put down?

Mortgage lending separates borrowers into prime and subprime categories. Prime borrowers have virtually no credit problems, strong income, and lots of cash in the bank. They are also called "A borrowers." Everyone else is subprime and is rated from A– down to D.

To see how you rate, check the ratings that follow.

Note: The ratings below are unofficial guidelines that are intended only to suggest what lenders typically look for. Each lender has its own yardstick.

What Kind of a Borrower Are You?

Rating	Description
A	Most creditworthy. Fit underwriter's profile (described below). Credit score over 700. (Nearly 60 percent of all applicants fit into this category.)
A-	One unpaid bill, under $1,000, turned into collection or no more than one late payment of over 60 days or two late payments of over 30 days in credit cards or installment debt all within the last two years. No bankruptcies or foreclosures on record (at least for the previous seven years). Credit score over 680.
B	Within the past year and a half you have had a few late payments of no more than 30 days in credit cards or

installment debt. You may have had a bankruptcy or a foreclosure concluded at least two years before you applied for the loan. Credit score of above 600.

C   Within the past year you have up to six late payments of no more than 30 days in credit cards or installment debt. You may have accounts currently in collection, but mortgage may be granted if they are no more than $5,000 and paid in full by the time the mortgage is funded. Mortgage funds may be used to clean up these debts. If you have a bankruptcy, it was resolved at least a year before you applied for the mortgage. If you had a foreclosure, it was concluded at least two years before you applied for the loan. Credit score below 600. (Only about 15 percent of all applicants fit this category.)

D   You have many current late payments, have several accounts in collection, and have judgments against you. These can be paid off from the proceeds of the new mortgage. If you have a bankruptcy, it was concluded more than six months before you applied for the new mortgage. If you had a foreclosure, it was concluded at least two years before you applied for the loan. Credit score below 575.

How Do You Stack Up?

If you're a prime A candidate, read on. The material immediately following is designed to show you how lenders might evaluate you for the amount of down payment, loan amount, and whether or not you'll actually get the financing. If you're B or lower, you may want to check later in this chapter where you will find there are mortgages available for you, too.

Note: For this chapter, we are only going to talk about institutional lenders, such as large banks and mortgage bankers, and large secondary underwriters, such as Fannie Mae and Freddie Mac. The rules we'll describe here do not apply to individuals, such as an individual seller making a home loan to a buyer.

TRAP

There are many vagaries in mortgage lending. You can be an excellent credit risk, yet by doing something as simple as having too many credit cards (even if you don't have any balances on them), you can lower your score. On the other hand, you may be a terrible credit risk, but by presenting your credit information in just the right light, you may secure excellent financing.

In the old days (say, about 15 years ago, before computerization took hold in the field) you could pretty much tell the size of a mortgage you were getting by using a couple of simple formulas. Add in a good credit report, and you were home free.

Back then, basically, if you put 20 percent down, your monthly mortgage payment couldn't be much more than a little above a quarter of your gross income. If you put 10 percent down, it couldn't be more than a little less than a third. If you had the right percentages and a clean credit report, you would get your mortgage.

Do You Fit the Profile?

Not so anymore. Today's institutional lender uses a sophisticated financial "profile." Like the profiles that supposedly identify terrorists at airports to ticket agents, these profiles supposedly separate for lenders the good credit risks from the bad. They are based on hundreds of thousands of mortgage lending case histories. Essentially what the underwriters (those who ultimately determine whether a mortgage is worth the risk or not) have done is to statistically compile the characteristics of low- to high-risk borrowers. The result is the profile.

If you fit the profile of a low-risk borrower, you get the loan. If you're off a bit, you might have to come up with more cash and get a smaller loan amount. If you don't fit at all, you can't get the mortgage.

TIP

Remember, we're talking here about prime or A loans. In the next section we'll discuss subprime or A– and lower mortgages, which may be more easily secured by those who don't fit the profile for prime loans.

In today's world, who gets the top mortgages is a matter of fitting the right profile.

Note that the profile of a low-risk borrower is drawn from statistical case histories. That means that anomalies may be introduced.

For example, statistically, a low-risk borrower won't have more than three credit checks by lenders (not including those where you check your own credit) in the previous six months. (Whether or not the credit checks reflect actual money borrowed isn't relevant.) If you—or anyone—applies for four or more, you could be out of the profile and may be disqualified. Yes, this practice is arbitrary and almost capricious, since in the real world you might have shopped for a car, stopped at half a dozen dealers to make offers, and each of them might have run a credit check on you. And you may not have bought any car or borrowed any money! Nevertheless, the statistics show that more than three credit checks in six months means added risk. Go fight the system!

Basically, when you apply for a mortgage you are asked to fill out a standardized application, which identifies a whole series of categories, including the following:

- Your income
- Your expenses
- The amount of cash you're putting down
- Where you're getting that cash from
- Your reserves (money in the bank)

The lender then determines additional information from a credit report, including the following:

- Your history of repaying borrowed loans
- Your current outstanding debt
- How long your credit history is

Based on how you score in all of these areas, you will or will not be granted a new mortgage. Or you may be granted the mortgage *if* you put down more cash and get a lower mortgage amount.

Let's consider some of the individual categories.

How Big Are Your Income and Your Expenses?

Your income is obviously how much money you make before taxes. It includes such things as receiving alimony. If both spouses have a long history of career work, their entire salaries may be counted. On the other hand, if one spouse works only part time or has only a short work history, just a portion of his or her income may be counted. Your expenses include PITI (principal, interest, taxes, and insurance) on the property plus living expenses plus other debt.

TIP

When you fill out a mortgage application, do *not* lie about anything. However, when you are explaining income, it usually pays to emphasize length and continuity. For example, you're a teacher who just a month ago has gotten his first job in years. The lender is bound to wonder if you will succeed at the work. However, if you note that you were a teacher with five years' experience a decade ago before leaving the field to help raise children, it puts your application in a whole new and better light.

The method by which you receive your income is important, too. If you work for an employer and receive wages (meaning you receive a W-2 form at the end of the year), you get preference mainly because it is easy to verify your income and because, presumably, you have something called "job security." (The only way a lender can determine this is by asking your employer what your chances for future employment are—a question frequently asked!)

On the other hand, if you're self-employed, you may be turned down without further consideration. Some prime loans will not be granted to self-employed individuals. In other cases you will be asked to produce your 1040 federal tax filings for the previous two years. The concern here is actual verification of your income. (You could submit false records, although now many lenders are capable of verifying income directly with the IRS!) And when you are self-employed, unless you can show a long work history, you are presumed to be at risk of job loss. See Chapter 8 for more information on how to better present yourself on a loan application when you're self-employed.

The amount of your income will have to be big enough to allow you to make the mortgage payments plus have sufficient monies left over for all your living expenses plus your taxes. Complex formulas for "front end" as compared to "back end" are used. Front end is the ratio of your house payment, including principal, interest, taxes, and insurance, to your income. Back end is the ratio of your total family payments to your gross income. I've found that these formulas are beyond the interest of most consumers, and besides, they aren't at all helpful to most borrowers when they are trying to figure out if they will qualify for a mortgage. Suffice it to say that you need as much income as possible.

TIP

If possible, pay off any short-term debt, such as credit card debt, *before* applying for a mortgage. That way you increase your income; less is set aside to pay for the short-term debt, thereby increasing your chances of qualifying. On the other hand, the more of your available cash you use to pay off debt, the less you will have available for a down payment and closing costs. Again, it's a trade-off.

How Much Cash Should I Put Down?

How much cash you put down depends on your perspective. For most home buyers/borrowers, putting down as little as possible is usually a good idea. That's certainly the case if you want to leverage your investment.

From the lender's perspective, the bigger the down payment, the better. The reason is that the larger the amount of your own money you invest in the property, the less likely you are to let it go to foreclosure if the market turns down or you lose your job. Presumably, the more money you have in the home, the harder you'll fight to keep it.

Another consideration is where you get the money. Ideally it will be your own money earned over the years and set aside as savings. Borrowing the down payment is a no-no. It suggests to the underwriter that you really can't afford the property. Let the lender know you're borrowing your down payment and you almost certainly will be scuttling the loan.

TIP

If you borrow money that you intend to use as part of the down payment, do it well in advance of applying for the mortgage (at least six months). That way, the money will be seen as part of a savings account, and the loan will be long established. In other words, you won't be borrowing specifically to make the home purchase.

Gifts from relatives are usually acceptable. These must, however, be legitimate gifts. They can't be given with strings attached, such as you'll repay them at the rate of so much a month and when you sell the property you'll repay the balance in full. In that case, they are nothing more than a disguised loan.

TRAP

 In the past, many underwriters insisted that those offering gifts as part of the down payment and closing costs cosign the mortgage and also qualify for it. This stipulation effectively nixed the deal in many cases. That requirement, however, has been removed for many federally underwritten mortgages. Today, a gift with a simple gift letter may suffice. Check with your lender.

How Much Should I Have in Reserve?

Reserves mean what you have left in the bank after you make the down payment and take care of the closing costs. Ideally, lenders would like to see at least three months' worth of monthly expenses. If you have only a month or two in reserves, you could be turned down or, more likely, may be asked to arrange for a smaller loan.

In the real world, more important than a few meaningless months of reserves is your ability to generate income and to secure additional borrowing (from lines of credit, credit cards, and so on), should something untoward occur (such as illness or job loss). If you can continue to generate income one way or another to meet your monthly housing expenses, who cares how much you actually have in reserve? The underwriters care, because it's part of the low-risk profile!

What Is Your Creditworthiness?

This is the critical question, and it is broken down into many categories. It includes your payment history, the amount of your outstanding debt, how long you've been borrowing, the number of inquiries, and the kind of credit you use. We'll consider each.

TIP

Lenders get all of this information from a credit report. For a mortgage, this is a special report that usually covers the three national credit reporting agencies:

TransUnion   www.transunion.com
Experian (formerly TRW) www.experian.com
Equifax   www.equifax.com

A three-bureau credit report is obtained, and it usually reveals everything there is to know about you. If you ever held out any hope of concealing bad credit, forget it. If it's there, the underwriters will find it.

What Is Your Payment History? The credit companies check the public records to see if you have had any bankruptcies or foreclosures. They also look for any loans you have that are now in collection.

The credit agencies also try to determine whether you are delinquent in any of your trade lines (credit cards). Any adverse notation can be cause for not issuing the mortgage.

TIP

If you're behind in payments, catch up *before* applying for the mortgage. Try to stay caught up for at least three months before applying so that your delinquencies will show up as old rather than recent. Old delinquencies are much easier to forgive. However, be aware that frequent and severe delinquent payments can also sink you even if you're caught up now. The best policy is to preserve your good credit by always paying on time. If you can't make the payments, don't borrow the money.

TRAP

A recent bankruptcy can sink you. However, if it's been seven years or more, it may simply be ignored by the lender. A discovered foreclosure, however, is almost never ignored. Lenders don't like to offer mortgages to people who have in the past allowed their homes to sink into foreclosure.

What Is Your Outstanding Debt?   What are the recent balances on all of your trade lines (credit cards)? The average balances over the past six months? How close are you to your credit limits?

The underwriters are concerned about people who live on their credit. They don't mind if you borrow, as long as you have plenty of credit left. On the other hand, if you have 10 credit cards and are borrowed to the limit on all of them, it suggests a poor money manager—and someone who might not be able to make mortgage payments.

TIP

If you are borrowed out, before applying for a mortgage, consider paying down or at least consolidating some of your outstanding debt. Perhaps you can obtain a single loan that will not only pay off all existing debt but also leave you a considerable buffer of unused credit. It will certainly look better to your mortgage underwriter. But do it well in advance (at least six months) of your mortgage application.

How Long Have You Been a Borrower?   Lenders want to know that you've been successfully borrowing for a long time. That tells them that you're a good money manager. To determine this, they look at your oldest trade line. The older the better.

TIP

Hang on to old credit cards. Keep a credit card that you have had for years even if a new credit company offers you a somewhat better deal. That old credit card shows that you have a long history and may help you get your mortgage. This is the case even if you just keep the card in a box and almost never use it.

How Many Recent Inquiries Have You Had and New Accounts Opened?   We covered this subject earlier. More than three credit checks in six months usually is a mark against the borrower. Yes, this practice is irrational, but go argue with a profile.

Similarly, if you open too many new credit cards or other charge accounts, it looks suspiciously like you may be planning to borrow a lot of money and leave the country. The underwriters check your most recent new account. An account opened in the previous three months is not good.

What Types of Credit Do You Have?   A good balance between credit cards, car loans, personal finance companies, and other installment loans is best. You don't want a lot of any of these or even a huge total. But the fact that you've got a car loan, three credit cards (the ideal amount, no more no less), and perhaps a department store card and you've maintained reasonable balances all suggests you're a good credit manager. And that's what the underwriters actually want to see the most.

Who Actually Sizes You Up?

The credit reporting agencies simply report. The underwriters often don't have time for the detailed analysis required to come up with the profile. That leaves it up to a different kind of company to take a look at your overall credit picture and see where you fit. Those companies are called "credit scorers." They include CreditXpert (experian.com), PLUS Score (consumerinfo.com), and the best known of the group, FICO (myfico.com), which stands for Fair Isaac Corporation.

For a fee to lenders/underwriters, FICO and the others will examine your overall credit background and then give you a score based on a rating scale, generally between a low of 350–400 and a high of 850. The higher your number, the more chance you have of getting a mortgage. The lower your number, the less your chance.

What's Underwriter Approval?

The underwriters look at your credit score and also at other items we discussed earlier, such as the amount of your down payment, your income, and your reserves. If all of these fit their own profiles (you're A or A–), chances are you'll get the loan.

If they don't, and you still have a reasonably good credit score, chances are you won't be turned down flat for a new mortgage. Rather, you'll be given a conditional approval provided that certain conditions are fulfilled.

These conditions may be something as simple as providing missing documentation such as a W-2 form or an old paycheck stub. Or they might be something more severe. The underwriter may feel that in order for you to meet the profile, you must increase your down payment and, accordingly, reduce the amount you are borrowing.

That's a lot to ask. You may not have any more cash and may need the maximum loan. If that's the case, the answer could be, "sorry."

Should You Get Discouraged?

Remember, at the beginning of this section I said that we were considering prime A mortgages. These go to the very best borrowers, those with sterling credit and lots of cash. In other words, people who probably don't need the money in the first place!

But, if you get turned down, there are a tremendous number of other mortgage alternatives available, including getting a subprime loan, a subject considered next. In other words, if you're given a hard time, don't get upset. Don't get discouraged. You can get a mortgage. You may just have to dig a little deeper.

Subprime Mortgages

If you're subprime, don't take it as a criticism. It merely suggests that you're human, that once in a while you forget or can't make a payment on time. That's not a terrible crime or even a moral issue. For many of us, it's simply a fact of life.

And it shouldn't and doesn't mean that you can't get a mortgage. In many cases, particularly if you're a B borrower (see above), you can. Indeed, many of the prime lenders now offer mortgages to the best subprime borrowers. The only difference is that they may charge an extra point or two or the interest rate may be higher.

Your best bet is to check with a good mortgage broker, although you can go online and use a good search engine such as Google and use the keyword *subprime*. You should find hundreds of lenders who are ready to offer you financing. The following lenders were apparently involved in subprime loans at this writing: New Century Financial, Ameriquest Mortgage, Full Spectrum Lending, Option One Mortgage, and Fremont Investment & Loan.

TIP

You'll end up paying more in interest and points for a subprime mortgage. On the other hand, you'll still be able to get a loan. A few years ago, it was almost impossible for subprime borrowers to get real estate financing.

TRAP

There is a tendency for some lenders to "stick it to" subprime borrowers. The worst cases of lending abuses, including excessive "garbage fees," occur in the subprime category. Be careful. Don't necessarily accept the first terms you are offered, particularly if they seem onerous. Check around.

How Much Extra Will It Cost for a Subprime Mortgage?

The answer depends on what category you're in. The lower your category, the higher the interest rate. If you're C or below, you may have trouble finding any kind of institutional lenders. (Although, you may get a seller to finance the purchase of his or her home for you!)

If I'm Subprime, Can I Assume a Mortgage?

One of the most underused techniques of getting a mortgage when you have some credit problems these days is to assume an existing mortgage. An "assumption" means that you take over the responsibility for making payments and ultimately paying back an existing mortgage. Someone else got the mortgage at some time in the past. It's currently on the home you are buying. You now take it over.

Unfortunately, assuming a mortgage in today's world is often more difficult than it sounds. The reason is that most lenders today prohibit assumptions. The mortgages contain an "alienation" or "due on sale" clause which effectively keeps you from taking them over. The minute the property is sold, the existing mortgage must be paid off in full. Thus, you can't assume it.

However, there are some mortgages that remain assumable. We'll cover three.

VA Loans. In general, you can assume an older VA mortgage. However, unless you're a veteran and also qualify for the mortgage, you don't really assume personal responsibility for repayment. That remains with the original borrower. If you don't make the payments and default on the mortgage is declared by the lender, you can walk away virtually free. The original vet who borrowed the money, however, will be held responsible for the VA loan. For this reason, many vets won't let others assume their loans. Or if they do, they will require the new owners to sign a notice of assumption that's filed with the VA and that transfers responsibility for repayment. However, if you're not a qualifying vet, the VA may not go along. (See Chapter 16 for more details on VA loans.)

FHA Loans. Some early FHA loans are still freely assumable. More recent loans, however, require that the new owner qualify for the mortgage as if applying for a new loan. The trick is to find one of the older, fully assumable mortgages.

ARMs. Adjustable rate mortgages are also often assumable. At the time of the sale, however, the mortgage frequently jumps up to current interest rates, and the new buyer must qualify as if for a new loan. Hence, the value of the "assumability" is questionable.

TRAP

One of the biggest problems with assuming an existing mortgage is that often it is only for a fraction of the purchase price. Typically, these loans were put on the property years ago and since then prices have gone up (and the mortgage has gone down as it's slowly been paid off). As a result, the assumable loan may be only for 50 or 60 percent of the sales price.

TIP

A way around this problem is to get the seller to carry back a second mortgage for another 20, 30, or more percent of the sales price. This raises the total mortgage amount to a level where the buyer need only put 10 or 20 percent down. Further, most sellers rarely require the buyer to qualify. Thus, your subprime rating doesn't enter the picture at all!

What about Equity Financing?

This is a totally different approach to getting a mortgage. Here, you don't qualify, the property does. Equity lenders, in fact, don't care what your rating is. They typically don't even order a credit report!

What they do order is a strict appraisal of the property. Then they offer a mortgage that is typically between 60 to 70 percent of the appraised value. The interest rate also may be higher than that of a conforming prime loan, and there may be more points to pay. But, even if you have D credit, you may be able to get this kind of a mortgage.

TRAP

Some equity lenders are in reality simply looking to acquire good real estate. They are actually hoping that you will not make the payments and default so that they can foreclose and get the property. That's one of the reasons they make the interest rate high and charge more points, to make it more difficult for you to succeed.

TIP

Before securing an equity loan, do a very careful financial analysis of your situation. Make sure you really do have the wherewithal to make the payments. You don't want to put a lot of your hard-earned cash into the property only to discover later on that you can't hang on to it.

Where Can I Find an Equity Lender?

A mortgage broker may be able to recommend one, but often brokers don't handle this type of financing. Rather, check in the yellow pages of the phone book under "mortgages." Look for ads that say something like, "We don't care about your credit!" or "We'll loan to anyone." That should get you headed in the right direction.

What Is an Asset-Based Mortgage?

An asset-based mortgage is like an equity mortgage only it's for people who have a lot of money in the bank. You want a mortgage, but you have terrible credit or don't want anyone looking at your credit *and* you have a lot of savings.

So, you approach your banker and explain your situation. You ask for an "asset-based mortgage." If the banker is agreeable, you get a mortgage based mainly on your savings (although the lender may also insist on a mortgage covering the property). Typically the interest rate is very low, and there may be no points at all to pay.

TRAP

Be aware that this type of mortgage ties up your savings. The bank probably won't allow you to make significant withdrawals on the asset given as security until the mortgage is either significantly paid down or paid off.

You'll get this type of mortgage primarily from banks. The bank in which you currently have your savings is the first place to look. If it's unwilling, check with other banks, indicating you'll make a substantial deposit into savings *if* they will grant the mortgage. This is an inducement few bankers can overlook.

What about Seller Financing?

As noted briefly above, in this situation the seller is your lender. As part of the purchase price, you ask the seller to carry back either a second mortgage (where you get an institutional first or do an assumption as noted above), or a first mortgage for the full borrowed amount.

Also see Chapter 15 for more details on how to arrange for seller financing.

TIP

In order for the seller to be agreeable, he or she usually must have either a large equity in the home or have a home that's fully paid off. This allows the seller to carry back the mortgage paper. You probably won't be able to work this deal with sellers who only have a little equity in their property.

Quick Quiz—Rate Yourself

Answer the following questions to see how likely you are to be seen as an A borrower by an underwriter. Note that the following quiz does not qualify you—only an underwriter can do that. Further, the questions are only approximations. For example, if you put less than 20 percent down but have good reserves, you may still get the mortgage. Other factors, such as your FICO score, also apply. To find out if you actually do qualify for a loan, check with a mortgage broker or other lender.

1. Are you putting at least 20 percent down?   Yes [ ] No [ ]

2. Will the total loans be no more than 80 percent of the purchase price (in case you have a second mortgage)?   Yes [ ] No [ ]

3. Is your gross income at least 3½ times your total monthly payment?   Yes [ ] No [ ]

4. Do you have little to no outstanding debt running six months or longer?   Yes [ ] No [ ]

5. Do you have enough cash in reserve so that after paying the down payment and all closing costs you will have at least three months' worth of expenses in savings?   Yes [ ] No [ ]

6. Do you work for an employer (not self-employed)?   Yes [ ] No [ ]

7. Have you been caught up in all of your credit card and installment debt payments for at least two years?   Yes [ ] No [ ]

8. Do you have no trade lines in collection within the past five years?   Yes [ ] No [ ]

9. Have you had no bankruptcy within at least
   the past five years?   Yes [ ] No [ ]

10. Have you had no foreclosure within at least
    the past 10 years?   Yes [ ] No [ ]

11. Do you have at least, but no more than, three
    trade lines (credit cards)?   Yes [ ] No [ ]

12. Have you had no more than three credit
    checks within the past six months?   Yes [ ] No [ ]

13. Are your credit card balances no more than
    half of your total credit line?   Yes [ ] No [ ]

14. Is your oldest trade line (installment or
    credit card) at least two years old?   Yes [ ] No [ ]

15. Are your current housing expenses roughly
    equivalent to your new housing expenses?   Yes [ ] No [ ]

If you answered yes to *all* of the questions, chances are excellent that you will qualify for the lowest interest rate prime loans. On the other hand, if you answered no to one or more questions, you might still qualify. Remember, only a lender can tell you for sure—and only after you've filled out and applied for a mortgage.

7

Can I Improve My Credit?

The kind of mortgage you get, and in fact, whether or not you can get a mortgage at all, hinges on your credit—your credit report and your credit score. Have good credit and everything will move along splendidly. Have bad credit and things becomes much more difficult.

Obviously good credit is desirable, but what if you already have some bad credit? Is there any way you can make it better? That depends on what the trouble is. It's a mistaken belief that you can have all bad credit "fixed." Companies that offer to fix or make any credit problem disappear, particularly if they charge you a hefty fee for doing it, could be nothing more than scams. Be wary of credit "fixers."

In this chapter we'll consider some options you may have to legitimately improve your credit, or what to do if you have little to no credit at all (a horse of a different color).

TIP

Pay your bills on time. Nothing messes up your credit quicker than late payments. Yet, these often result from carelessness or forgetfulness. Keep all bills in a special spot and make it a point to pay them at least once a week. This is probably the simplest yet most effective step you can take toward preserving your good credit.

TRAP

If you find that you're unable to pay all of your bills, at least make your mortgage payment. If there's only one bill that you can pay, be sure it's your mortgage. Foreclosure and late mortgage payments are the only things that mortgage lenders are very reluctant to forgive.

Can I Explain Away a Problem?

Yes, sometimes you can, particularly if it's a good explanation. Lenders are human too and they realize that sometimes creditworthy people get into trouble. If your explanation shows that you at least tried to solve the problem and, perhaps even more important, that the problem was isolated and isn't likely to happen again, you may very well be able to get the financing you want, even a prime mortgage!

The best way to do this is to be up front with the lender. Don't wait for the problem to surface as part of your credit report. Get it out front. And provide the lender with a clearly written letter of explanation. If you have late payments, explain why they were late. If you defaulted on a loan, give all the details and include verifying information. If you had a foreclosure, explain how it occurred and why circumstances are different now.

It's a good idea to get a copy of your own credit report in advance of applying for a mortgage. That way, you get to see what the lender will see and be able to prepare for it. You are allowed to obtain at least one copy of your credit report each year. You probably will want to get it from one of the big credit reporting agencies. The cost is typically minimal, around $10. The three big agencies are

TransUnion	800-888-4213
Experian	888-397-3742
Equifax	800-685-1111

TIP

You should be able to get a copy of your credit report free, once each year. This capability has been mandated by Congress in the 2004 Fair and Accurate Credit Transactions Act. Thus, AnnualCreditReport.com

(877-322-8228) was established. You may call or e-mail and, after providing enough information to indicate who you are, you can receive back a credit report from the repository you designate. (It's usually a good idea to not provide personal banking information, such as account numbers or locations, or sensitive financial information.) In theory, you can use the service three times a year by requesting separate reports from each agency.

Some Explanations a Lender Might Accept

In the past almost all lenders were willing to accept a written explanation for bad credit. Recently, however, many lenders have begun refusing to even look at such explanations. If you have credit that needs explaining, ask your mortgage broker for a lender who accepts an explanation.

You Were Unemployed or Sick for a Period of Time. This explanation may be acceptable if you have a long history of excellent credit broken by a short period, say six months, of poor credit, followed by another long period (a year or two) of good credit. This explanation is particularly helpful in explaining late payments.

You Had a Divorce or Death in the Family. Here again, you normally must show that this event happened some time ago and since that time, you've had excellent credit. This explanation is particularly useful when you defaulted on loans. You had a big setback in your life, but now you're back in the saddle, as evidenced by at least two years' worth of good credit history.

The Bad Credit Is Someone Else's Fault. This is not a great excuse, but it's a plausible one. Perhaps you cosigned for someone else on a car. That person ran off with the car and never made the payments. You were stuck with either making payments for five years on a car you didn't have and couldn't sell or simply refusing. You refused.

This explanation shows you had the good sense not to get in debt over your head. But it also shows that you had the bad sense to cosign for someone else. Further, given tough circumstances, instead of plodding on and making payments, you'll bail out—something that makes good sense to you but which lenders don't particularly like to see.

You Got in Over Your Head.   You live in California, but bought property out of state just before the real estate recession of the mid-1990s. You couldn't sell or rent it and weren't there to take care of it. Consequently, you lost it to foreclosure.

But that was years ago and it was on rental real estate. Here and now you're trying to buy a home in which you plan to live. The circumstances are different. Maybe the lender will agree.

You Were the Victim of a Natural Disaster.   There was a hurricane (or earthquake or fire or whatever) that destroyed not only your home but also the factory where you work. You had no place to live and no way to earn income. Naturally, you had to let your house go into foreclosure. But since then the factory is rebuilt and you're back at work. You're ready to start again buying a house.

All are good answers. Will they satisfy a lender? Maybe. It's worth a try, and if doesn't work, try a different lender.

What If the Credit Reporting Agency Made a Mistake?

I have heard reports that as many as a third of all credit reports contain an error of some kind. Often these errors can cause you to be declined for a mortgage. When that happens, you need to get out and correct that error. (This is another good reason to order your own credit report early on. You can discover if there are errors and take steps to correct them.)

Generally speaking, the best approach to take in correcting an error is to obtain proof that it is indeed an error and then write to the credit reporting agency offering the proof and demanding that the error be corrected. The credit agency must investigate your request and take action, usually within a month or two.

The trick is getting the proof. What's usually accepted is a letter or document from the lender that reported the bad credit saying it was a mistake. Or, in the case of mistaken identity, it's a matter of presenting irrefutable evidence that you're who you are and not the other person the credit company thinks you are. Birth certificates, a driver's license, escrow company ID statements, and so forth can help in this situation.

On the other hand, sometimes the problems are just plain weird. Consider this example: I ran into an individual who sold his home and gave the buyer a second mortgage. That buyer eventually defaulted and the seller was forced to start foreclosure on the second. To protect his interest in the property, he began making payments on the existing first mortgage. He found, however, that the property had been so destroyed by the previous owner, that it had fallen in value to the point where it wasn't worth foreclosing. (The market was not booming at the time in his area.) So he stopped making payments on the first mortgage and simply took a complete loss on the second.

When the first mortgage went into foreclosure, however, because he had temporarily made payments on it, he was erroneously listed as a borrower and the credit reporting agency put a foreclosure against his name. He discovered this error when he applied for a new mortgage and was turned down by the lender.

What he had to do was to contact the lender of the first mortgage and secure an explanation from that lender and take that information along with all the documentation from the original second as well and present that to the new lender. Once the new lender understood the situation, his mortgage was approved.

If the borrower had first submitted summaries of all of this information to the credit reporting agency, he might never have had problems with the new lender. *Note:* the credit reporting agency may not accept your explanation, no matter how convincing. The originator of the bad credit report—the lender—may have to contact the credit reporting agency directly to have the mistake removed.

TIP

The basic method of correcting bad credit is twofold. First, you have to write a letter explaining the problem and why it wasn't your fault. Second, you have to submit documentation proving what you say.

Will the Credit Agency Correct the Mistake?

That depends on your proof. If the original lender who reported the problem now reports an error, the agency will normally remove the offending report.

On the other hand, if your proof tends to be your word against the lender, who refuses to admit an error, it's a different story. The credit report agency may insert your letters of explanation along with the bad report and may make your substantiating documentation available to those who ask for reports.

The credit agency, however, doesn't usually take sides. In a disputed case, they probably will not remove the offending incident. It will stay on your report usually for around seven years.

For more information on how to correct an error in your credit report write to:

Federal Trade Commission/Division of Credit
Consumer Response Center
Room 130, Sixth St. & Pennsylvania Ave., N.W.
Washington, D.C.   20580
202-382-4357 (FTC-HELP) www.FTC.gov

What If I Have No or Little Credit?

Having no credit is almost as bad as having terrible credit. In order to give you a mortgage, a lender has to establish your money management patterns. It does so by seeing how successfully you've paid back money that you've previously borrowed. But, if you've never borrowed, the lender can't establish a pattern. And in the world of borrower profiles (explained in Chapter 6), that can leave you out in the cold.

That doesn't mean, however, that you can't otherwise establish your credit and get a mortgage. Indeed, having no credit can be just an inconvenience. If you make the proper efforts, you can establish a good credit record and be years ahead of the individual who starts off with lots of bad reports.

Where Do I Begin to Establish Credit?

Begin at least six months but preferably a year or more before you plan on applying for a mortgage. It will take time to establish a good credit history. It can't be done overnight. Here are some suggestions:

First thing, go to the bank where you do business. (Not having credit doesn't mean you don't have a checking and savings account.) Apply for a debit card. As you probably know, this is like a credit card, only based on your assets in the bank. Today, many banks offer these cards virtually automatically to their customers.

Once you have the debit card, use it frequently, establishing that you can manage such an item. Also, be scrupulous to see that you never bounce your own checks and can always cover any checks from others that you deposit. Ask your bank to establish a small line of credit to cover your checking account, just in case you should be short. This overdraft credit line is also often just done automatically for good, long-standing customers.

Once you have an overdraft account and a debit account, ask your bank for a credit card. Almost all banks offer them. With your good standing in the bank, approval should be automatic.

Once you get that credit card, you're halfway home. Go out and charge halfway to the limit. Then pay it back promptly. Pay off all your charges each month for three months and you've established a preliminary credit history.

Very shortly, other credit card offers should start appearing in the mail. Apply for two others (no more, no less). Charge a few things on these and make regular monthly payments.

Now, go back to your bank and ask for a noncollateral loan—a line of credit. Say you want to buy furniture or a used car. You have your history at the bank, plus your new credit cards, plus the fact that you have no bad credit. Again, it's a slam dunk. Borrow a thousand dollars or so this way, put it in the bank, make regular payments on it, and after a few months, pay it back.

Voilá—with the exception of longevity, you have just established the rudiments of prime credit. Age means how long you've had your trade lines. That first credit card you got? Keep it. It will age, and once it's two years old, you've satisfied the age portion.

TRAP

Make all of your payments on time! Remember, you want to establish good credit, not bad.

What If I Need to Establish Credit Instantly?

The above plan is great *if* you've got the time to spend. But, what if you want to get a mortgage right now? You don't have time to set up credit cards and installment loans. You want to buy a home and you have to go with what you've got. But you have an empty credit history.

Actually almost no one's credit history is truly empty. At worst, it's usually just a case of not having thought of what to fill it with.

TIP

Some lenders have begun processing applications of those with little credit history using information such as that supplied here. Check with a good mortgage broker to see who's offering this when you apply.

Here are some suggestions for creating an instant credit history:

Rent Receipts.   You must have lived somewhere, and if you didn't own, you rented. If you paid rent by check, get those canceled checks. They should show a steady pattern of regular payments. Better still, get a letter from your current and previous landlord stating that you made your rent payments on time. Also have the landlord state the monthly payment, to establish that you can handle such a large amount.

Utility Receipts.   You had to have electricity, water, garbage, gas, phone, and probably cable TV. You paid for these. Again, look for canceled checks. Also, call up the companies and ask them for a letter of recommendation. Many utility companies will do so almost automatically if you've had a good payment history for one year.

Informal Loans.   People who don't use formal credit often get loans from friends and family. If you paid these back on time, get your canceled checks or other receipts. Have the person sign a statement showing the amount borrowed, the term, when regular payments were made, and when it was paid back. If the person from whom you borrowed the money is able to put a corporate or business name on the statement, even better.

You might need to dig into your memory for some other account that also can be used to help establish your credit. Dig as deeply as possible. While none of these individually is as good as a long history of credit cards with prompt repayment, they can go a long way.

Should I Consider a Cosigner?

You certainly can. If you don't have the credit history, you can try to find someone who does and ask her or him to help you out.

Relatives are usually opportune choices. Good friends, even business associates, are also possible candidates. Remember, hopefully you don't need the cosigner to help you with the down payment or the monthly payments. You just need his or her good, established credit.

TRAP

When someone cosigns with you, his credit is on the line. If you default, or worse, if you lose the property to foreclosure, it will reflect badly on his credit. It will be as if he were late on payments or lost the property. For this reason, keep in mind that most savvy people will refuse to cosign for anyone, even close relatives.

To induce another person to cosign for you, you may want to give her an ownership position in the property. You may want her to have her name appear both on the deed and on the mortgage. That way, should you for some reason stop making payments or go into foreclosure, she could step in and take over and possibly save the property. This can be a strong inducement to a reluctant cosigner.

TIP

Most lenders will want the cosigner on the mortgage in any event. So, it's just a simple step more to include him or her on the deed.

TRAP

Once cosigners are on the deed, they can tie up the property and potentially keep you from selling. To protect your interests, you will want to have an attorney draw up an agreement specifying exactly what interests they have (presumably none, except in the event you default), what say they have in managing or selling the property (again, presumably none, unless you have a problem), and what percent of the profit they will receive in the event the property is sold (again, presumably none). This agreement will help protect, but not guarantee, your interests.

8

Mortgages for the Self-Employed— No-Doc Loans

As you may have discovered, it's harder for the self-employed to get a mortgage. There are basically two reasons for this. First, it's difficult to get documents that spell out a self-employed person's true income. Second, lenders worry that in their eagerness to get financing, the self-employed may be less than completely forthright on those documents that are used (such as 1040 tax forms). Less-than-honest answers can be very difficult to detect.

On the other hand, with a salaried individual, a pay stub or a letter from an employer will usually suffice. After all, that employer (presumably an uninterested third party) is usually handling tax withholding and paying social security taxes; hence, the chances of false statements on salary forms are greatly reduced.

Nevertheless, it is possible for the self-employed to get a good mortgage, even in a fairly straightforward manner, in many cases. We'll see how in this chapter.

How Do I Prove My Income If I'm Self-Employed?

The answer has traditionally been to submit two years of federal 1040 income tax returns. These returns show on Schedule C the income and expenses of the self-employed person as well as the bottom-line take-home pay.

TIP

> While you may only be asked for two years of tax returns, the lender is looking to see that you've been self-employed for many, many years to show that you are successful in your business endeavor. The longer you can show you were successfully self-employed in the same field, the better.

The problem with showing tax returns, however, is that often they don't reflect the true income of the self-employed. For example, there's the matter of SEP-IRAs or Keogh plans. Money placed into these areas is subtracted from the borrower's taxable income. However, most lenders are adept at adding back these amounts, so the problem is largely one of perception rather than reality.

A more real problem, however, is the fact that some self-employed individuals actually take home a great deal more than their tax returns show. This is particularly the case in cash businesses.

But even where all income is declared, it may be reduced significantly by items such as depreciation on equipment or home expenses that appear primarily on paper, not in reality. Lenders really can't add back in depreciation and home expenses, since they are counted as expense items. So, what is a self-employed individual to do when he or she can't demonstrate enough income to qualify for a mortgage, even though he or she actually has a large income?

Until fairly recently there really wasn't a good answer here. However, in the past few years mortgages without documentation have come into existence. They have solved a lot of problems for the self-employed.

TRAP

In desperation to get financing, don't be tempted to submit a false tax return to a lender. While the lender may accept it initially and even issue a mortgage based on it, that tax return stays with your mortgage file forever. If you ever default on the mortgage, the tax return will be dragged up and you may have to get proof from the IRS that it was authentic. Not being able to do so could be considered fraud in applying for a federally regulated mortgage and could result in severe criminal penalties. Further, today many lenders are connected directly to IRS files and can electronically call up your true tax return!

What Are Mortgages without Documentation?

These loans go by a variety of names from low-doc to no-doc to NINA (No Asset Verification Arm) to "liar's loans!" They simply do not require much documentation. There are no verifications from employers or banks. No two or three years of tax returns.

The way they work is that you submit your name (and necessary information to prove who you really are, such as a social security number) and the property address. You allow the lender to run a credit check and get a credit score on you. You do *not* have to supply any proof of your income, your assets, or your bank accounts. Based on what you submit, a lender then issues you a mortgage for the amount you want.

Of course, there is a catch—several catches. First, the mortgage often carries a higher interest rate, often 1 or 2 points higher than market. Second, the borrower may be required to put more money down instead of the usual no-down or very-low-down payment. Finally, there also may be more points to pay than for a documented mortgage.

Further, if the borrower later defaults and it turns out that false statements were originally made, the penalties could be severe. It's not something to take lightly.

Nevertheless, especially for the self-employed individual who has trouble showing as much income as he or she actually makes, this type of mortgage can be a godsend. It provides the opportunity to get a mortgage to buy a home simply on a signature.

Unfortunately, while the first wave of no-doc loans were issued with relative abandon a few years ago, a large number of them went into default during the real estate recession of the mid-1990s, and the entire process fell into disfavor. If you want a no-doc loan today, you may have to look a bit harder to find a mortgage broker who handles it.

TIP

Don't aim for a no-document mortgage. A documented mortgage will usually provide a lower interest rate, lower costs, and a lesser down payment. Even if you are self-employed and cannot show on tax returns as much income as you feel you make, you may still be able put enough paperwork together to get a good documented mortgage.

Other Alternatives for the Self-Employed

If you bank regularly with a particular institution, contact them. For a good depositor, they may be willing to make exceptions.

I have a friend who was recently in this situation. He went to his local small bank, where he did over $2 million a year in business, and asked for a $300,000 home loan. When he couldn't come up with the required documentation, the bank turned him down. He then notified the bank president that he was turning the bank down by taking his business elsewhere.

Talk about a turnaround. His mortgage was funded within the week!

9

Can I Cut My Mortgage Costs?

Just like death and taxes, there are almost always costs when a mortgage is obtained. In most cases, you will be asked to pay these costs out of pocket, and they will be in addition to whatever you put as a down payment. But in some cases these costs can be folded into the loan, as we'll see shortly.

Unfortunately, some of the costs you'll be asked to pay may be "garbage fees," costs that are unjustified by the service performed by the lender. These garbage fees, unfortunately, have increased over the last few years as interest rates have fallen or remained low. These costs do not benefit you but instead go toward the lender's or the retailer's bottom line. In this chapter we're going to examine the various closing costs you may be asked to pay and try to separate the chaff from the wheat.

Is There Any Government Protection for Me?

In 1974 Congress passed the Real Estate Settlement Procedures Act (RESPA). This act grew out of the many abuses that some lenders had perpetrated on home buyers/borrowers.

RESPA requires specific disclosures from lenders at different times. It also works to prevent lenders from getting kickbacks from other parties to a transaction. Your first contact with it will be when you fill out an application for a home mortgage with a lender.

The lender is required by RESPA to provide you with a "good faith estimate" of the costs involved in closing the deal, the settlement costs. This estimate must be mailed to you within three working days of receipt of your loan application.

What Is the Good Faith Estimate?

The good faith estimate should include all of the costs that can be estimated by the lender. These include points and other fees but do not include prorations for taxes and insurance, which cannot be calculated until the close of escrow. You should also get the annual percentage rate (APR) statement, which is the true interest rate (as calculated by the government) you will be paying for the mortgage.

TIP

Be aware that these are only estimates, sometimes very rough estimates. Your actual costs will not be known until the close of escrow.

TRAP

The APR will usually be different from the quoted rate for the mortgage. Don't be misled by this. The APR takes into account all of the costs, including points, that go into your interest rate. The stated interest rate of the mortgage is just that. The APR is what your effective interest rate will be.

The whole point of the good faith estimate is to allow you some time to shop around. Since it is given so soon after you make the application, you should have time to reject that lender and find another, should you choose to do so. The lender is obligated to attempt to hold to the terms listed in the good faith estimate when the final documents are drawn.

What Other Disclosures Will I Be Given?

There are many other disclosures usually given at closing. One that will catch your eye indicates whether or not the lender you are dealing with will actually be the one to service your loan (collect the money). Oftentimes lenders will sell the rights to service the loan to other companies. In most cases this won't have much effect on you.

Another disclosure is the "affiliates" disclosure. Pay attention to this. A lender or a broker may refer you to someone else, such as an escrow or title insurance company, to handle the closing of your deal. If this is the case, then you are required to be given an "affiliated business arrangement disclosure." This form lets you know that in most cases you are not required to go with the lender (or broker's recommendation), but may shop around on your own for the best deal.

Yet another disclosure is your HUD-1 statement, which is a true and accurate account of all the costs of your transaction. However, it does not have to be given to you until one day before the loan closes.

In 2003 Congress passed the Fair and Accurate Credit Transactions Act (FACTA). It requires that the lender inform you if the lender's profiling system (called a "risk-based pricing system"; see Chapter 6) came up with a negative finding that's resulting in a higher interest rate to you. You can dispute this finding and try to get a lower interest rate loan.

TIP

In some states the seller may not compel the buyer to use a particular closing agent as a condition of the sale. This enhances your opportunities to search for the best price.

All of these disclosures as well as others are helpful to you as the borrower. But they alone do not guarantee you're getting a fair deal.

TIP

One of the worst feelings is to walk into an escrow company to sign documents only to discover that the mortgage isn't as it should be. You can avoid this problem by demanding that the lender or the person handling the closing, show you the HUD-1 settlement statement *one business day before the closing.* Granted, one business day is not a whole lot of time. But if there is something significantly wrong, it does give you time to alert your agent or attorney and, if necessary, to hold up the close of escrow.

What Can I Do If I Find Something Wrong?

By the time you're ready to close escrow, you are going to find it very difficult to hold up the deal for a small problem (such as an unwarranted cost) with the loan. To do so might jeopardize the entire transaction with the seller. In other words, at this point it's probably too late to argue about a cost that you think is unfair. (That should be done when you are first given your good faith estimate at the time you apply for your mortgage.)

What you can argue about, however, is a cost that appears on your settlement statement that did not appear on your good faith estimate (exclusive of prorations). If you think there is an unjustified cost here, let the lender, agents, attorneys, and everyone else know. You can be sure that every attempt will be made to explain the cost to you and it may turn out to be perfectly justified. Or it may turn out to be a mistake. Or it could be something else.

When Should I Check Out the Costs?

You should check them out when you are given your good faith estimate, within three days of filling out a mortgage application. The chances are very good that many of the fees, warranted and not, will be listed here. If you're going to argue about them, now's the time to do it. (*Note:* Usually lenders will list industry standard costs. However, by the time the deal closes, some costs could be higher or lower.)

But, you may wonder, how can I complain? The lender represents a giant institution. It sets the rules by which the game is played.

Not necessarily. Keep in mind that the lender wants your business. Point out a fee you think is completely unjustified, and if the loan broker or other loan officer you are dealing with can't justify it to your satisfaction, it may be taken off. The lender knows which fees are justified and which aren't. You complain about an unjustified fee and it might get removed.

Or you can walk away. If you don't like the fees the lender is charging, find a new lender. The power of choice is ultimately your best weapon.

What Are Typical Mortgage Settlement Costs?

Here, then, are your typical mortgage settlement costs.

Appraisal Fee

The lender sends out an appraiser to give a written estimate of the property's value. This estimated value is what the mortgage is based upon. The cost of the appraisal will vary enormously. It might be as inexpensive as $75 and as costly as $350. However, since the lender picks the appraiser and sets the charge, your only two choices are to pay it or get a different lender.

TIP

An appraisal is a necessary part of the mortgage lending process, and you will be told that it is customary for the borrower to pay for it. That's true. However, there is nothing to keep the lender from absorbing this cost if it wants to. In a tight market with lots of lenders and few borrowers, some lenders will offer free appraisals. It's something to shop for.

Assumption Fee

If you are assuming an existing mortgage, the lender will probably charge a fee for handling the paperwork. This fee is usually around $100.

Attorney's Fees

If you have an attorney, you can expect to be charged a fee. However, if the lender has an attorney, you may be charged a separate fee.

There is no reason you should have to pay for the lender's attorney unless unusual work was performed. This should be a cost of doing business for the lender. You may want to challenge this fee.

Commission

Paid to the real estate agent, this shouldn't normally appear on the buyer's estimate-of-cost sheet. It could, however, if you used a buyer's agent or agreed to pay part of the seller's agent's fee.

Credit Report Fee

The lenders charge for a credit report. This fee usually is under $50, often $25 to $35. It is a normal and customary fee. You have to pay it, unless the lender agrees to absorb the cost, which some highly competitive lenders do.

Discount Points

This is a one-time charge. Each point is equal to 1 percent of the loan. Points are used to adjust the yield of the mortgage to correspond to market conditions.

TRAP

Some lenders charge points as a way of confusing you, the borrower, as to the actual interest rate you are paying. You think you are getting a low interest rate mortgage. But, when the points are added in, you may be paying above market! Your best bet is to shop around. Find the lowest rate *with* the lowest points.

Document Preparation

The escrow company will usually charge a fee, often under $50, for the preparation of documents such as the deed. However, some lenders will also charge an additional document preparation fee for preparing the deed of trust or mortgage. I have seen these fees range from $35 to $300.

This fee makes no sense at all to me. If the lender is giving you a mortgage, it should be a cost of business to prepare the mortgage document. I always challenge this fee.

Escrow Charges

The "escrow" is an independent third party who accepts all the monies, gets the deed prepared, and then actually handles the closing of the transaction. In the Midwest and West there are actual escrow companies (often the same company that issues the title insurance) that handle this matter. On the East Coast in some states this function is performed by an attorney. There is a fee for this service.

Again, shop around. You normally aren't bound to use any particular escrow company that a lender recommends. You can use the one that gives you the best price.

Hazard Insurance

You will be required to provide a fire and hazard insurance policy to protect the lender. Typically, you must pay for these policies at least one year in advance into escrow. However, the policies are written for three years, and some insurers require all three years paid in advance. Check with your insurance agent.

Impounds

If your mortgage was for more than 80 percent loan-to-value ratio, you will probably be required to impound taxes and insurance. Setting up this account requires a "cushion." What this means is that the lender will collect a portion of the money for taxes and insurance from you in advance and then pay them when due. The lender should collect a couple of months of insurance and taxes in order to get this account started.

TRAP

In the past, some lenders collected as much as 6 to 12 months' worth of payments in advance, then put the money into their own account and received interest on it. This practice was halted when RESPA required the lenders to collect *no more than two months'* worth of insurance and taxes for the impound account.

Also, be aware that some lenders charge a separate fee for setting up the impound account and yet another fee for administering it. These last two, to my way of thinking, are unjustified.

TIP

If your mortgage is for 80 percent loan-to-value ratio or less, you can ask that instead of an impound account, you be allowed to pay your own taxes and insurance. The lender usually will do this, unless there is some sort of problem (such as you have bad history of managing such monies). If you handle the taxes and insurance yourself, you will have a much lower monthly payment. *But* you will have to come up with lump-sum monies to pay for taxes and insurance at different times during the year. If you opt for this, be aware of your saving and budgeting habits. It only works if you're able to save the money on your own to pay taxes and insurance when they come due.

Interest

You will be obligated to pay the interest from the date of the closing to the first monthly payment.

TIP

Unlike rent, interest on a mortgage is paid is arrears. Thus, if you can arrange to have the escrow close on the last day of the month, the next payment won't be due until the first day of the month after next. This means you won't have to pay any interest into escrow and you'll have a whole month before your first payment comes due.

Lender's Title Insurance

Most lenders will require a separate, more comprehensive and more expensive policy of title insurance. This is frequently required because of underwriting. You'll simply have to pay it.

Mortgage Insurance Premium

For an FHA loan, this has to be paid all in advance into escrow. For private mortgage insurance, the amount may be for several months in advance, to cover the payment in the event you default on the mortgage.

Origination Fee

This is a charge to cover the lender's administrative costs in processing a loan. It was standard with FHA government-insured loans.

With conventional loans it is often expressed as a point or perhaps a few hundred dollars plus points. For example, a particular mortgage might be 2 points plus $350. The $350 may be the origination fee, or one of the points may be it. It goes to pay a mortgage broker for getting the loan or a loan officer for processing the loan.

To my way of thinking there is little justification for this fee in a conventional loan. The lender is getting the interest—that should be sufficient. If there are other administrative costs, the final lender should advance these and the interest rate should be adjusted accordingly. However, almost all lenders do squeeze in a few hundred dollars as a way of milking you of additional money when obtaining a mortgage.

TIP

If the fee is under $350 and if it's a good mortgage, you may be just as well off paying it. On the other hand, if it's higher, then you will certainly want to shop elsewhere.

Title Insurance

In most cases you will want title insurance in order to protect your title. I would never buy property without title insurance. The fees for this insurance vary slightly. Remember, in most cases you don't have to go with the title insurance company the lender may recommend. Check around for the best rates.

In addition to the costs listed above, there could be additional charges that may or may not be reasonable. You'll have to use common sense here or check with your real estate attorney.

The time to challenge lender's fee is as early as possible. If you don't like a fee, ask the lender about it. If the explanation isn't adequate, ask that the fee be removed. If the lender refuses, consider finding a different lender.

What about a Prepayment Penalty?

A prepayment penalty is just what it sounds like. It's a penalty for paying off a mortgage earlier than its due date. The payment amount varies, but sometimes it can be substantial, running into the many thousands of dollars. You may want to check the documentation of your mortgage to see if it includes a prepayment.

As a buyer, prepayment comes into play because today most mortgages do not include it. As an enticement to include a prepayment clause, lenders will sometimes offer a cash incentive, typically anywhere between $500 and $2,500 when the mortgage is made. Accept the cash and have a penalty for paying off the mortgage early.

TIP

If you're quite sure you're going to live in the property a long time, it may make financial sense to accept a prepayment penalty for which the lender offers a cash incentive. After all, you'll be getting the cash for nothing! Just be sure that there's a time limit on the prepayment penalty, typically five years. After that, there should be no penalty. Also, keep in mind that if your plans change, it could cost you money!

TRAP

The money bonus offered by lenders is often much smaller than the penalty. For example, if you're offered $1,000, the penalty could be $2,500 if you pay off the mortgage anytime in the first five years. If your plans change or if you plan to sell the property or refinance, accepting this offer probably would make little sense for you.

Unfortunately, most people don't check until they're ready to close escrow on a sale or refinance. By then it may be too late.

Check out your mortgage documents, if you're not sure, before you put your house up for sale or before you begin the refinancing procedure. A hefty prepayment penalty may lead to a change in your plans.

What If I Want to Complain about a Lender?

At any time, you can complain about a lender's actions directly to HUD, which administers RESPA. You should be aware, however, that HUD, rather than look closely at individual complaints, tends to investigate those lenders who have had a whole battery of complaints leveled against them.

If you want to complain, write out a statement of the problem and include copies of all supporting documents. Send them to:

U.S. Dept. of Housing and Urban Development Director
Office of Insured Single Family Housing
Attention: RESPA
451 Seventh St. S.W.
Washington, D.C. 20410

Also check to see if there are any agencies at the state level that likewise supervise lenders. You may have an even better chance of getting help there.

A Great Booklet to Check Out

HUD also prepares an excellent booklet, "Buying Your Home—Settlement Costs and Other Information." It is available from HUD or may be downloaded (in a variety of formats) from HUD's Web site: www.hud/gov/fha/res/stcosmsw.bin. It is the best-prepared booklet on settlement costs that I've ever seen.

10

How Can I Cut My Mortgage Payments?

I've never met anyone who didn't want to reduce his or her mortgage payment. Unfortunately, when the consequences of making that reduction were explained, the person sometimes declined. Yes, you can cut your payment. But, do you really want to?

There are three factors influencing the monthly payment:

1. The size of the mortgage
2. The interest rate
3. The term

In this chapter we'll look at four methods of reducing the monthly payment mainly by manipulating either the term or the interest rate.

1. Balloon payment
2. Buy-down
3. Adjustable rate mortgage (ARM)
4. Convertible mortgage

A fifth method that's obvious is that you can cut your monthly payment by reducing the mortgage amount by increasing the down payment.

Using a Balloon Payment

A "balloon" in real estate finance is nothing more than one payment of a mortgage (usually, but not always, the last) which is bigger than any of the others.

The balloon payment has been talked about so much (often erroneously and negatively) in the general press that it has achieved legendary proportions. However, there is nothing wrong with a balloon mortgage, as long as you, the borrower, understand it and know when that one payment is coming. In truth, the balloon payment is nothing more than a financial device that can be of benefit to the borrower. It's simply a matter of understanding when and how to use it.

TRAP

Be aware that many mortgages with balloon payments *do not explicitly state this fact.* Rather the mortgage might be written in such a way that it only specifies interest and term. It leaves it up to you to figure out whether or not a balloon is involved. Ask your lender, your agent, and your attorney if you're not sure.

What Are 5/30, 7/30, or 10/30 Mortgages?

Any mortgage can have a balloon payment. It's simply the way it's written. One of the most popular mortgages as of this writing is the 5/30. In this mortgage, the payments are amortized (paid out) over 30 years. However, the entire mortgage is due in five years. In other words, there is a balloon of all the unpaid balance at payment number 60.

The purpose of this mortgage is to give you a lower monthly payment. This is possible because, from the lender's perspective, this is actually a five-year loan (you owe the balance in five years). This relatively short term affords the lender less risk over time than a 30-year payback and, thus, you get a lower interest rate and payment.

TIP

Varieties of this mortgage offer payoffs at years 3, 7, 10, and 15. These are known as 3/30, 7/30, 10/30, and 15/30 mortgages. The shorter the payoff term, the lower the interest rate.

For example, on a straight 30-year mortgage for $100,000 the interest rate might be 7½ percent. However, on a seven-year mortgage, since the exposure for the lender is much shorter, the interest rate might only be 7 percent. (The actual spread will vary, depending on market conditions and the lender's goals.) The difference in payments can be significant:

30-year mortgage at 7½%   = $699
30-year mortgage due in 7 years at 7%   = $665

You save $34 a month. Keep in mind that if the entire mortgage were to be amortized (paid off in equal payments) in just seven years (no 30-year amortization), the monthly payment would jump to $1,324.

TRAP

Be sure you're clear about what a 5/30 mortgage really is. It's a 30-year loan with a balloon payment at year 5. That means you need to come up with cash at the end of five years either by refinancing or by selling the property.

TIP

Don't assume you can always refinance when the balloon payment comes due. Five years from now your financial condition may be far different. There could be a recession and you may have lost your job. You may not qualify for a new mortgage, and if you couldn't refinance the balloon, you could lose the house to foreclosure. Always insist that the 5/30 have a rollover clause. This means that at the end of the five years it automatically rolls over into another mortgage, typically an ugly adjustable rate mortgage (explained below) with a high interest rate. Never mind about the type of mortgage. You just want to be sure that should your financial situation change, you can always get some kind of loan to protect your home.

What Is a Buy-Down?

The buy-down is not so much a particular kind of mortgage as it is a tool that can be used with any kind of mortgage (with the lender's cooperation) to lower your *initial* monthly payments.

In a buy-down you end up with a lower interest rate for the first years of the mortgage. A typical buy-down is a 3/2/1 (see the table below). Here, the first year your interest rate is 3 percent below market, the second year it is 2 percent below, and the last year it is 1 percent lower. Your monthly payments are correspondingly lower as well.

Buy-Down Example

$100,000 @ 6 percent for 30 years: 3/2/1 buy-down

	Interest rate	Monthly pmt.
Year 1	3%	$422
Year 2	4%	477
Year 3	5%	537
Year 4 -30	6%	600

Who Gets Charged for the Buy-Down?

It's important to understand that in a buy-down there is no money that is actually saved. The lender still collects the full interest rate. The only difference is that instead of it being paid monthly, it is paid in advance.

In order to get a buy-down, someone must pay a willing lender additional points up front. The more points that are paid up front, the bigger the buy-down. (The actual number of points required to lower the interest rate 1 percent per year will vary with market conditions. Check with your lender.)

The most common example of a buy-down occurs when you are buying a brand-new home from a builder. The builder may advertise, for example, 3 percent interest for the first five years.

That, of course, is an extremely shocking advertisement in an era when 5 or 6 percent mortgages are already low. It is almost guaranteed to get buyers flocking to the builder trying to buy those properties.

But, how does the builder really offer such a low interest rate mortgage? Is that builder somehow tied into an exceptionally altruistic lender?

What the builder does is go to a lender and negotiate a mortgage for the buyers. The builder gives the lender a certain number of points up front, perhaps 5 or more. In addition, the lender may require an adjustable or higher-than-market fixed-interest rate after the first five years. The builder has paid the lender to lower the interest rate. The actual interest rate on the mortgage may be 5.5 percent. But the builder has "bought down" the rate on the first five years to 3 percent.

Of course, the money has to come from some place. Consequently, you as the buyer of the home, can expect to pay a higher price. (Of course in a cold market, the builder may be taking a sizeable amount of the cost out of its would-be profits.)

TIP

What's important to understand is that the buy-down does not mean that the mortgage costs less. It only means that someone has paid the lender to lower the interest rate so you can get a lower monthly payment.

TRAP

Money is money to the builder. If you would rather have a lower price and a current rate monthly payment, almost any builder will convert the buy-down to a lower sales price. Be sure that you calculate what is best for your own particular situation. You may find that you'd rather have a lower monthly payment than a lower-priced home!

What Are the Types of Buy-Downs?

The types of buy-downs are limited only by your imagination. We have already looked at the 3/2/1, as well as where the interest rate is kept artificially low for a period of years. You can tailor-make a buy-down to suit your particular needs. You can have a 1/1/1/1 (1 percent lower for four years) or a 2/3/1 (2 percent lower the first year, then 3 percent, then 1 percent). Or you can buy down the interest rate for the entire term of the loan. (This is usually expensive and adding points may only buy down the loan by a quarter percent or so at a time.)

Lenders are limited only by their ability to resell the mortgage in the secondary market (and their own conservativeness). If you are a truly qualified buyer, a creative lender should be able to calculate out the points needed to buy down any amount for any mortgage.

TIP

Anyone can buy down a mortgage: you, the builder, or a reseller. It just depends on who is willing to pay the points.

What Is an Adjustable Rate Mortgage?

In the beginning there was the fixed-rate mortgage. This simply meant that the interest rate remained the same for the life of the loan. If your initial interest rate was 6 percent, you paid 6 percent in year 7, in year 15, in year 22, and in year 30. The rate never changed. The fixed-rate mortgage is easy to understand. It makes sense. It's what made residential real estate so widely owned and so popular in this country.

Adjustable rate mortgages, or ARMs, are different. Here the interest rate charged to the borrower fluctuates roughly in response to the cost of funds for the lender. Your monthly payment could, for example, be low when you get the loan, higher a year later, and much higher a few years after that. The reason the monthly payment would go up (or go down) would be that the interest rate charged on the loan might go up (or down).

Perhaps an example will clarify just how an adjustable rate mortgage actually works. Let's say we obtain a mortgage of $100,000 at 8 percent interest per year for 30 years. If this is a fixed-rate loan, our interest will remain at 8 percent for the full 30-year term. Also, our monthly payment will remain at a fixed $734.

On the other hand, if this is an ARM, our interest rate may fluctuate up (for example, up to a maximum of 12 percent) or down (for example, down to minimum of 4 percent) over the term of the loan. With an ARM, the interest rate charged is adjusted up or down at regular intervals. Similarly, our payments may fluctuate widely, in this case, between $367 and $1,023.

What's the Big Advantage?

In order to induce borrowers to take out an ARM, lenders offer a lower-than-market initial starting rate (called a "teaser" and discussed in detail in the next chapter). The corresponding payments are lower. Thus, if you can't qualify for a fixed-rate loan, you might very well be able to qualify for the same mortgage if it were adjustable with lower initial payments.

TRAP

The big plus of a fixed-rate mortgage is that we always know where we stand. Our payments don't vary. On the other hand, the big plus of an ARM is that, at least initially, the payments are always lower than for a fixed-rate mortgage.

Besides a low initial teaser rate, ARMs also have the advantage of always being available. In times of volatile interest rates, such as back between 1978 and 1982, lenders such as savings and loan associations and banks, were afraid to lend money long term. They didn't want to commit themselves to a 30-year real estate loan when they had no idea where interest rates would be even six months into the future.

Thus, while lenders were quoting fixed rates of 17 percent (to protect themselves), they were also quoting ARMs of 12 percent. (Yes, that's very high when compared to today's rate, but low for their time.) They felt comfortable with the ARM because they knew that if interest rates in general rose, the rate on the ARM would also rise. Thus, when fixed-rate loans are difficult or impossible to find, ARMs are usually plentiful. For detailed information on ARMs, see Chapter 23.

What's a Convertible Mortgage?

A convertible mortgage is something like a convertible car—it has two different modes. With a convertible car, you can have the top up and, thus, drive a conventional automobile. Or, you can lower the roof and have a sporty open-air vehicle.

A convertible mortgage also has two modes. In one mode it is a staid conventional type of loan. In the other it has sporty adjustable rate features.

The convertible blends adjustable and fixed features. You can get the big advantage of the adjustable rate mortgage—lower initial interest rate—but you can also achieve increased stability over the life of the mortgage. For the lender, the convertible is a compromise. It doesn't lock the lender into a long-term fixed rate, which could be catastrophic if interest rates rise. On the other hand, it doesn't give the lender quite as much protection against volatility as the straight adjustable rate mortgage.

TIP

The convertibles are some of the better mortgages available for borrowers. However, you have to shop carefully, since they come in all sizes and shapes, and some can be quite ugly.

How Does a Convertible Mortgage Work?

A convertible mortgage is really like two mortgages packaged together. In one popular form, you start out with an adjustable rate. Then, after a preset number of years, you are given the option of converting to a fixed mortgage (at then-current market rates).

For example, you might have an adjustable rate mortgage with a low initial rate. It would be like any other ARM except that at, perhaps, year 3, you could convert it to a fixed mortgage at the then-current market rate, at your option. Of course, you might have to pay a "conversion fee" to do this.

Once again, the big advantage of a convertible is that it's a way to get a lower interest rate and, thus, a lower monthly payment. The lender gives a lower rate because the mortgage is adjustable. Yet you get the opportunity to convert to a fixed-rate mortgage later on. Most lenders offer convertible mortgages of one sort or another.

TRAP

Be sure you understand how and when the conversion operates. In some mortgages you only have a small window of opportunity to convert, say between years 4 and 5. Further, if interest rates happen to be high during the conversion window, you won't want to convert—and you'll lose your opportunity after the window; the loan then usually remains an ARM for the rest of its life.

TIP

The value of a convertible loan comes from your ability to convert it to a fixed rate at some time in the future. If the conversion window happens to be during a period of lower interest rates, you can get into a fixed mortgage for very little in costs.

11

Introduction to No-Down Payment Mortgages

Can you buy with nothing down? Yes!

Should you? Sometimes!

In the past many gurus have touted buying with nothing down as a formula for success in real estate. Buy with nothing down, get the property of your dreams, and make a fortune to boot.

Unfortunately, it doesn't always end up that way. A lot depends on how the financing is structured. If you end up with payments that are sky-high, it might be a formula for disaster. You wouldn't be able to make the high payments and could lose the property to foreclosure.

On the other hand, if you can arrange for a low interest, nothing-down mortgage, it's another matter entirely. After all, if the market rate for a conventional loan with 20 percent down is 6 percent and you can get almost the same interest rate for 0 percent down, why not go for it?

What Is LTV and CLTV?

It's important to remember that virtually all mortgages are based on the market value of the property. They are a certain percentage of that value expressed as "loan-to-value," or LTV. For example, a mortgage for 80 percent of value is expressed as an "80 percent LTV."

Sometimes in order to get closer to no-down, two mortgages will be combined, a first and a second. For example, the first might be for 90 percent and the second for 10 percent, adding up to 100 percent of the market value. These mortgages are expressed as "combined loan-to-value," or CLTV. The two mortgages described above would have a 100 percent CLTV. In general, most lenders are very hesitant to issue mortgages where either the LTV or the CLTV is more than 90 percent. But it can be done—read on.

Are You a Prime Borrower?

True nothing-down financing has become available only within the last few years. These are mortgages for the entire purchase price from institutional lenders—the same people you go to for the 20 percent down loans.

In the past, any loan that was underwritten (by Fannie Mae or Freddie Mac) had to have at least 10 percent and preferably 20 percent down. This was to insure the lender that the borrower would be dedicated enough about the property to keep up the payments.

However, as we saw in Chapter 6, the big lenders no longer use the old formulas for finding good buyers. Today it's all done on the basis of a computer profile. If you fit the profile of the good borrower who would never let a property go into default, then it shouldn't make any difference if you put 20 percent down or nothing down.

As a result, the major underwriters have begun fielding a variety of programs that offer up to 100 percent loans. If you qualify, you don't need to put any money down (or very little). Fannie Mae has, for example, a program called the "97" that requires a borrower to come up with only 3 percent down. On another you not only don't come up with any down payment, but 3 percent of your closing costs are covered, to boot. Other zero-down programs are currently being offered. To find out about such programs in effect when you're reading this, contact your mortgage broker.

What about Government Loans?

In addition, there are the FHA and VA loan programs. These offer low (typically 3 percent on FHA) or nothing-down (on VA) loans to qualified buyers. Again, you must be a strong borrower and, in the case of the VA loan, you must also be a qualifying veteran. (See Chapter 16 for more details.)

The problem with these government mortgages, however, is that they have relatively low maximums. This means that while they are adequate for moderate-priced areas, they are irrelevant in high-priced housing markets. As of this writing, however, the government has been toying with the idea of boosting the maximum loan amount on both of these mortgages to the same as for conforming (Fannie Mae/Freddie Mac) loans, which is currently $359,650. Check with a lender, such as a bank, to see what the current maximum is.

What about Closing Costs?

It's important to understand that the down payment is not the only cash you need to come up with in a real estate transaction. There are also the closing costs, which include appraisal, credit check, recording fees, and, of course, points.

With an FHA mortgage, the closing costs, including points, can typically run to more than 5 percent of the mortgage. And the FHA wants these fees paid up front, although in some cases they can be financed as part of the mortgage.

On a Fannie Mae or Freddie Mac underwritten loan, the cost can be similar. Under other programs, it can, however, be much less, as little as 2 percent. And again, in some cases it can be included in the loan package.

You should check with your lender to see what the actual closing costs are. With zero-down mortgages, often the closing costs are the only cash you need to come up with. And sometimes, as noted, even a part of these can be financed into the mortgage.

What If I'm Not a Prime Borrower?

Not everyone is a prime borrower who can fit the qualifying profile for many of these zero-down mortgages. If you're not a prime borrower, is there any opportunity here for getting such a loan?

Yes, of course there is. There is always seller financing, which used to go by the term "creative financing." In many markets, particularly when sales are slow, it is possible to get the seller to help you finance a portion of the purchase price, sometimes enough so that you don't have to put anything down. We'll cover this in detail in Chapter 15.

If you don't want or can't put anything down, today you may still be able to buy a home. The finance industry has been turned on its heels by the computerized profile system, and it could produce surprising results for you. Just ask your lender about nothing-down mortgages. There may be one just waiting for you out there.

12
Can I Cut or Eliminate Points?

Over the last few years some mortgage lenders have been offering to lend money with "no points" to the borrower. Points, as you may recall, are a percentage (1 point equals 1 percent) of the mortgage amount that goes back to the lender. A zero-points mortgage means that the borrower pays no points at all. Should you look for and obtain one of these special mortgages?

First, let's be clear on what we're considering. You want to borrow $100,000 to buy or refinance a home. You go to lender after lender and are told it will cost you around 6 percent in interest plus anywhere from 1½ to 2 points in the then current market. In other words, there's an additional $1,500 to $2,000 in loan costs (in addition to settlement fees).

Suddenly another lender pops up and says if you borrow from it, there are no points to pay at all. You save the $1,500 to $2,000 it would otherwise cost you. Should you believe it? Should you jump for it? Yes ... and no. It depends on your situation. It could be beneficial, or it could end up being even more costly.

Do You Believe in the Tooth Fairy?

If you still believe in the tooth fairy, the Easter Bunny, and Santa Claus, then you're ready to accept that one lender will give you a mortgage for $1,500 to $2,000 less than another. (Maybe you're just such a nice gal or guy that the lender can't resist.) On the other hand, if you're an adult who's been burned once or twice, you'll look deeper and ask more.

In truth, the loan without the points can and may be more costly than the loan with the points. To understand how and why, it's important to realize why lenders charge points.

Why Points?

Lenders aren't concerned with interest rates per se. They are concerned with "yield." Yield is the true return to the lender on the money that is loaned. It includes not only the interest rate you pay but also all other costs and fees that can be factored in, especially points.

Thus, if you want to borrow $100,000, but pay 2 percent of the loan up front in points, you're actually only borrowing $98,000. Yet, your interest rate is based on $100,000. Since the lender loans you less (in this case $2,000 less), it receives a higher yield on the money.

TIP

Figure it out. At 6 percent, the monthly payments for 30 years on $100,000 is $600. However, if you pay 2 points, you're in reality only borrowing $98,000. If you make payments of $600 on $98,000, the true interest rate returned to the lender is actually close to 6¼ percent. Because you borrowed less but made higher monthly payments based on a higher loan amount, the lender gets a better yield.

Does it really work this way? Yes it does. And if you want further proof, consider the APR (annual percentage rate) that must be given to you when you borrow. This is somewhat higher than the true yield to a lender because it includes all mortgage costs. Nevertheless, you will notice that if you have costs including points, your APR will always be higher than your mortgage interest rate. It is closer to the true yield.

Trading Interest for Points

Now we can get to how a lender can offer a zero-points mortgage. It is done, quite simply, by jacking up the interest rate. You want to borrow $100,000 at 6 percent and the lender says it will cost you 2 points.

You say you don't want to pay 2 points. You don't want to pay any points. The lender is an agreeable sort and says okay. It's 0 points, only the interest rate is now 6¼ percent. Why shouldn't the lender be agreeable? The yield on either loan is the same. (If you're not sure why, reread the tip above.)

Thus, points can be traded for a higher interest rate. Indeed, many modern lenders will offer a sliding scale of points versus interest rate, such as the one shown below.

Sliding Scale—Points vs. Interest Rate

3 points	5⅞%
2 points	6 %
1 point	6⅛%
0 points	6¼%

It's your choice.

TRAP

Don't think that you can automatically trade 1 point for ⅛ to ¼ of the interest rate. While it often works out close to that amount, as we'll see shortly, there are other considerations that lenders have.

Should You Pay the Points or Pay a Higher Interest Rate?

The answer depends on your financial situation and how long you plan to live in the home. Basically, points are cash to you up front. If you're short of cash (as so many buyers are), then a zero-points mortgage can be a good deal. On the other hand, if you've got the cash and plan to keep the property a long time, then perhaps a lower interest rate (and accompanying lower payments) would be advantageous.

There's an additional consideration. Lenders aren't always equitable when they offer zero-points mortgages. By that I mean the trade-off between points and interest rate sometimes can favor the lender. Let's consider an extreme example.

You've got the choice between paying 2 points on a 30-year $100,000 mortgage or an increase of ¼ percent in the interest rate. That's either $2,000 in cash up front or $17 a month more. If you're short of cash when buying the home, that $2,000 can look like a lot of money. On the other hand, that $17 a month can seem a paltry fee. Yet, before you leap, consider that the mortgage is for 30 years.

$$\$17 \times 360 \text{ payments} = \$6,120$$

Over the 30-year life of the mortgage you will pay more than three times the amount you'll save on the points when you buy.

TIP

Calculate how long you must live in the property before you begin to lose money. In the above example, you'll stay ahead until about year 10. At that point you will have paid roughly an additional $2,000. Beyond that, it begins to cost you more money.

TRAP

Our example does not take into account the future cost of money, which means that cash up front is worth more (due in part to inflation) than cash received sometime in the future. Nevertheless, as a rough measure the preceding test works pretty well.

Problems arise when the lender is far less equitable than our example. Let's say, for example, that the choice is between paying 2 points ($2,000) up front or a ½ percent higher interest rate. Remember, the lender can charge any rate it wants, as long as it fully discloses that to you. (Some states still have usury laws against excessively high interest rates, but they usually do not affect institutional lenders such as banks.)

$$\$34 \times 360 \text{ payments} = \$12,240$$

Now, if you choose the much higher interest rate over the points, you're paying six times as much over 30 years. Your breakeven is in just roughly five years. (*Note:* Another way to make a determination is to calculate how long to break-even, as we've done here. Then, if you have a rough idea of how long you plan on living in the property, you can determine whether points or a higher interest rate is better for you.)

The Bottom Line?

Having said all this, how should you choose? Should you pay the points or pay the higher interest rate?

If it were me, I'd try to determine how long I planned to own the property. If I only plan to stay with the property for a few years, then I'd certainly want to take the higher interest rate (and monthly payment) and forgo the points.

On the other hand, if I planned on keeping the property a very long time, then it might be better to pay the points up front and take the lower monthly payment, as it would save me a lot of money over the long haul.

TIP

Sometimes interest rates fluctuate rapidly. For example, when you first look they could be at 6½ percent. A month later they're at 6¼ percent. When you finally apply for a mortgage they are down to 6 percent. Now you're given a choice of points over a higher interest rate. You might be offered 0 points at 6½ percent. But if you'd applied for the loan just a few months earlier, you would have paid 6½ percent even with points! All of which is to say that sometimes using a sharp pencil doesn't make much sense. If you can live with the interest rate and don't have the up-front cash for the points, you may just want to opt for the zero-points mortgage regardless of the long-term costs. (*Note:* The preceding logic works far less well when interest rates are rising.)

What about Zero-Cost Mortgages?

Sometimes lenders will offer you a mortgage at no initial cost to you at all. There will be no escrow charges, no title insurance costs, no settlement fees, and, of course no points.

Again, it's usually too good to be true. All of the other costs are part of getting a mortgage. If you don't pay them, then somebody else must. While the lender probably can cut a better deal with the title insurance and escrow companies than you can, nevertheless there will be some expense. And that expense will be added to the interest rate. In other words, you'll end up paying an even higher interest rate for a zero-cost mortgage than you would for a zero-points mortgage. Your monthly payments will be higher, as will the long-term costs.

Of course, as noted earlier, if you're only planning to live in the property a relatively short time or if interest rates have fallen to where you don't mind paying them, you may want to take a zero-cost mortgage.

13

What Is a Jumbo Mortgage?

What if you need a bigger loan than the "conforming maximum"?

Thus far we have generally been talking about lenders who are issuing "conforming" loans. This simply means that the mortgages conform to the underwriting guidelines and maximum loan amount used by the quasi-government secondary lenders, Fannie Mae or Freddie Mac (currently at $359,650).

But, what if you live in a high-priced area such as parts of New York or California? What if the average home in your area costs over $500,000 or, in some cases, over $800,000? How do you get financing?

Getting a Jumbo Loan

If you need a mortgage above the conforming limitation, you are now looking for what the industry generally calls a "jumbo loan" (up to $650,000—over that amount, they're "super jumbos"); currently that's any loan above $359,650. Suddenly you are in a different ball game.

The good news is that jumbos are readily available in those areas of the country where they are needed. The reason is that they are great loans, from the lenders' perspective, since the interest rate is often ¼ to ½ point or more higher than the conforming rate. The bad news is that they can require that the borrower have far more assets than for a conforming loan. (Super jumbo mortgages to well over $1 million with as little as zero down are available, but they require a great credit score and may cost even more in interest rates and points.)

TIP

"Jumbos" in the past have referred to mortgages of no more than $650,000. Those above this amount have been called "super jumbos."

Thus jumbos cost more for a lower loan-to-value ratio, or LTV. Plus, the lenders often adhere to the underwriting guidelines of Fannie Mae and Freddie Mac (even though the loan won't be resold), just to be sure that the borrowers are good credit risks. Thus the lenders get more interest for what some say is essentially the same risk.

Where Do I Get a Jumbo?

Most mortgage brokers, savings banks, or other lenders offer jumbos or can direct you to a lender who does. The procedure is essentially the same as for a conforming mortgage. You fill out an application, provide the required documentation, get an appraisal, and, if everything checks out, you get approved and funded.

It's important to understand, however, that jumbo lenders sometimes keep these mortgages for themselves rather than sell them in the secondary market. Thus, depending on the lender, it could take a while until the lender's own loan committee meets to get approval. If the committee meets only once monthly, it could take a long while to get approval.

Why Are They Also Called Portfolio Loans?

Sometimes the originating lender may not sell the jumbo to other lenders as part of a package (see below). Instead, the lender keeps the jumbo in its own portfolio of loans. Therefore, jumbos were originally referred to as "portfolio mortgages." There now is, however, a sort of private secondary market for these from lenders other than Fannie Mae and Freddie Mac (mainly banks and insurance companies).

Of course, the marketplace can only fund so many of these large mortgages until it runs out of funds. Hence, there tend to be fewer jumbos than conforming loans. On the other hand, there are also far fewer very high-priced properties.

Can a Jumbo Be in Any Format?

Certainly. A jumbo can be either a fixed-rate or an adjustable rate mortgage. It can be one of the popular 5/30 mortgages (a 30-year payout period [amortization] with a 7-year balloon). Or it can be a convertible loan. Currently one of the most popular jumbos is a "LIBOR," an interest-only loan tied to the London Interbank Offered Rate, or LIBOR.

There's almost no limit to the format the loan can take. Remember, the big difference between a jumbo and a conforming loan is the amount borrowed. The format of mortgage is a matter of agreement between you and the lender.

TIP

Since lenders often carry jumbo mortgages in their portfolios directly, they may have more flexibility than with conforming loans. That means you may be able to make specific offers regarding points, fees, or the LTV that they would entertain and, in some cases, accept. In other words, you may have greater flexibility in creating just the type of mortgage you want.

14

Should I Opt for a Biweekly Mortgage?

The long-term goal for most people is to eventually pay off their mortgage. While that may not make great financial sense (the interest is often deductible and the loan gives you greater leverage for making a profit on the property), it's often an overwhelmingly popular psychological motivation. As noted elsewhere in the book, nothing feels more secure than to have a paid-off house.

So, if you decide you want to pay off your mortgage faster, how do you go about doing it most efficiently?

What about a "Biweekly" Mortgage?

One of the most popular mortgages to be "discovered" in the last few years is the "biweekly." Here the borrower makes a payment every other week instead of the traditional once-monthly payment. (For example, instead of paying $1,000 a month, you pay $500 every two weeks.) Since there are 52 weeks in the year, a payment every other week amounts to 26 "half payments" or 13 full payments. (An extra $1,000 in our example.) With a biweekly mortgage, therefore, each year you make the equivalent of 13 monthly payments instead of 12. That thirteenth payment ($1,000 in our example) goes to pay down principal.

The result is that over the life of the loan an amazing amount of interest is saved and the mortgage can actually be paid off years early. In almost a painless way, you can thus cut virtually a third off the time it takes to pay off a 30-year mortgage.

TRAP

A biweekly mortgage is not for everyone. It works best when you are salaried and getting paid on a weekly or biweekly basis. You can more easily budget your money to take care of the payment that way and probably won't feel the extra expense very much. On the other hand, if you're paid monthly or work for yourself and receive income erratically, the biweekly setup can be a no-no. Making payments once each month will seem natural. On the other hand, a biweekly schedule will have you making payments more often, probably at times when you don't have money coming in. A biweekly schedule can be a nightmare for someone who is self-employed or who is paid monthly.

How Do I Establish a Biweekly Mortgage?

Biweekly mortgages are offered by many mortgage lenders. Just ask your mortgage broker to recommend a lender who uses them. They are set up right from the start with payment coupons that require you to make a payment every two weeks. The mortgage company takes care of the bookkeeping, and as long as you keep making those payments, you are shortening the term of your loan as well as the total interest you will have to pay.

TIP

A biweekly also can be used to reduce the size of your payments instead of shorten your term and cut interest. Say the payments on a 30-year mortgage are $1,000 a month and $500 biweekly. On a yearly basis paid monthly, you will have paid in a total of $12,000. However, biweekly that comes to $13,000. The extra thousand dollars can be used to reduce your biweekly payments by $42. Some lenders have encouraged borrowers to try this. However, keep in mind that this defeats the entire purpose of the biweekly. You might just as well pay monthly as to pay a reduced amount biweekly. You will not save anything on interest and will not have your mortgage term reduced. The only advantage I can see is for some borrowers who prefer lower biweekly payments as simpler for their book-keeping and budgeting.

TRAP

Beware of firms, particularly those that telemarket, that offer to set up a biweekly mortgage for you for a stiff fee. They could take your money, never make the mortgage payments, and cause you to lose your home.

I have seen companies that offer to set up a biweekly mortgage payment schedule with an existing lender when you already have a mortgage. They claim to call the lender and get an agreement to send in money every other week. In reality, some of these firms deposit the extra money in an interest-bearing account and then, at the end of the year, make an extra payment to principal. For this they often charge a whopping fee, sometimes as much as a $1,000 or more. Plus, they may require a biweekly charge for the service. They get interest on your money and a fee for doing what you can do yourself.

Can I Set Up a Biweekly Payment Schedule Myself?

You sure can. Ideally, a true biweekly mortgage is arranged between you and the lender at the time you secure financing. The lender agrees to accept payments every two weeks, and you agree to make payments on that schedule. If you already have a mortgage in place and a check with the lender reveals that no change in payment schedule is possible, you can still do it. Here's how:

1. First make sure you can make a prepayment without penalty. Most mortgages allow this, but some don't. Check your mortgage documents. If you're not sure, take them to a real estate broker or attorney who can explain them to you.

2. If prepayment is allowed, simply pay half your mortgage payment every two weeks into a separate checking account. At the end of each month, make your normal payment to the mortgage company out of that account. As the year progresses, you will notice a surplus slowly but surely building in that account.

3. At the end of the year, include that surplus with your December payment. *But be sure to indicate that it is all to go to principal.* If you don't, the mortgage company could simply count it as your next payment and mess up the entire schedule.

Keep in mind that you can accomplish the above on your own and very easily. You do not need anyone to help you do it. You certainly aren't required to pay anyone to set this up for you. But, to get a true biweekly mortgage, you must set up it up with the lender.

Why Not Simply Get a 15-Year Mortgage?

One way to pay more money up front is by taking a shorter payback period, 15 years instead of 30, for example. This increases the monthly payment but decreases the interest charged, resulting in a quicker payoff of the mortgage.

Comparison of 30-Year and 15-Year Mortgages

$100,000 @ 6 percent fully amortized		
	30 year	15 year
Total interest	$115,838	$51,894
Interest saved	...	$63,944

Note that by making a higher payment with a 15-year mortgage, you not only get the mortgage paid off in half the time but you also save a tremendous amount of interest.

Will I Have Higher Payments?

Of course, the problem with a 15-year mortgage is that it has higher payments. In our example of a $100,000 mortgage at 6 percent interest, that's an increase in the monthly payment of $244 ($844 rather than $600) on a 30-year mortgage. The payment increases by about 40 percent in this case. For most of us, that's too huge a burden to bear.

TIP

As we've seen elsewhere in this book, lenders like the shorter-term mortgages, because it reduces their risk. If you can afford the higher payments on a 15-year mortgage, a lender will often give you a lower interest rate or fewer points or both. That reduces your payment. It's something worth considering.

Still Don't Get How to Save Money by Paying Off Sooner?

It's all a matter of mathematics. Let's consider a fixed-rate mortgage. While we all understand that monthly payments on a fixed-rate mortgage remain the same, what fewer of us comprehend is the ratio of interest to principal in the payment.

During the early years of a mortgage, virtually all of the monthly payment goes toward interest. It is only in the very last years that the majority of the payment begins to go toward principal. Here is a graphic portrayal of a typical 30-year mortgage.

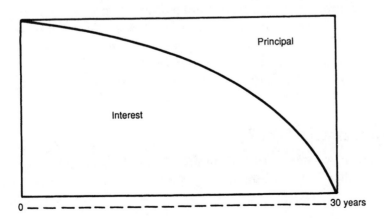

If the mortgage is for $100,000 at 6 percent interest over 30 years, the monthly payment is $600. However, of that amount only about $100 initially goes to principal on the first payment. All the rest goes to interest.

As you can imagine, reducing the $100,000 by $100 in the first month isn't going to make much of a difference. However, over time it adds up. Each month the mortgage interest is recalculated, and each month the amount that goes to principal increases while the amount going to interest declines. That's the reason that the curve begins to turn downward.

This steady increase in the amount going to principal continues over the life of the loan, but it actually begins to accelerate by year 15 (when $230 goes to principal). What's happening is that as the amount of money going to principal increases, the amount owed decreases and, consequently, the interest charged goes down. This process accelerates at the end of the loan period. By year 25 of a 30-year loan, you're actually paying more than half of the payment to principal and less than half toward interest ($419 to principal). By the final payments, virtually all is principal (final payment is $597 to principal).

What this means is that the vast majority of the interest paid on the mortgage over its life is paid during its first years. If you can reduce the principal in those first years, you significantly reduce the interest paid—and in the long run significantly shorten the time it takes to pay off the mortgage.

TIP

Simply making one additional monthly payment in the first year that goes entirely toward principal can reduce the time it takes to pay back the loan by over a year and significantly reduce the interest paid over the term of the mortgage.

Is There a Better Way?

I think there is a safer way. A variation of the 15-year mortgage that's been available for a long time is the 30-year mortgage paid back in larger monthly payments. No, it's not exactly a biweekly, but it's like it.

I can remember very savvy borrowers doing this as long as 30 years ago, often over the objections of the lender. Even back then, when most mortgages had prepayment penalties, they did allow up to the equivalent of six months' interest to be paid in advance, and people took advantage of that clause. Today with most mortgages not having prepayment penalties of any kind, it's even easier to do.

Here's how this plan works: You get a regular 30-year mortgage (with a no prepayment feature). But, you pay it off using a 15-year payment schedule. If you borrowed $100,000 at 6 percent for 30 years, your payments should be $600 a month. However, instead of paying $600 per month, you pay $844 a month—$244 extra going to principal.

30-year monthly payment	$600
Extra principal	$244 (prepaid monthly)
Total monthly payment	$844

What's the Advantage?

The advantage is you're not locked into the higher ($844 in this case) payment. You are paying it voluntarily. If you get laid off, if there's a problem such as sickness and you don't have any extra funds, or if anything else untoward happens, you just drop back to the old, lower ($600 in this case) payment. The lender doesn't care, since the lower payment is what you contracted for. Doing it this way, you have the option of making the higher payment or not. *You* determine which month you'll pay more and which you'll pay less.

Biweekly and 15-year mortgages are becoming increasingly popular, and for good reason. Borrowers are simply tired of paying huge amounts of money for interest over the life of a mortgage when, either by restructuring the frequency of the payment or by adding a small additional amount to principal each payment, they avoid that. Think of it this way: Paying every other week or paying an extra hundred bucks a month probably isn't going to kill you. But paying tens of thousands, sometimes hundreds of thousands, of dollars extra in interest over 30 years can be a real backbreaker.

TIP

You don't have to own the property for 15 years or longer to get the benefits of biweekly or 15-year mortgages. Everything that you pay immediately to principal increases your equity as soon as you make the payment. The sooner you pay or the more you pay, the lower the mortgage and the more of the house that you really own.

15

Can I Get the Seller to Finance Me?

"Seller financing," also called "creative financing," can be your source of the cheapest, no-qualifying, quickest-to-get mortgage money when you buy a home. In short, getting the seller to give you a loan is one of the best ways to get financing. If the seller is willing to give you a mortgage, either a first or more likely a second, you can get in quickly and without a lot of hassle.

TIP

For practical purposes, creative financing means seller financing.

In the past, creative financing became widely perceived as seller rip-off. The reason was that a few unscrupulous buyers and brokers connived to use this tool to cheat sellers out of their equities. So many sellers lost money that for a few years it was difficult for an honest buyer to get any seller to go along with it.

Today, however, most of the rip-offs are gone and many sellers are once again willing to help buyers purchase their homes. This is particularly true in areas of the country where the market isn't hot and sales aren't plentiful.

How Does Seller Financing Work?

As those familiar with real estate financing know, when a seller "carries back paper," he or she is creating a mortgage with the buyer as the borrower. The buyer, in essence, is loaned a portion of the seller's equity in order to be able to purchase the home.

TIP

The terms "hard" and "soft" money as applied to real estate have come into vogue. A soft money mortgage is one in which the seller is the lender. A hard money mortgage is where the buyer/borrower goes to a bank or institution for funds.

The most common form of seller financing is the second mortgage. Let's take an example of a seller's second. Helen wanted to purchase a home for $300,000. However, she only had $15,000 to put down (plus money for closing costs.) That meant that she would have to get a 95 percent mortgage.

The problem with this was that Helen couldn't qualify for the 95 percent mortgage. Her borrower profile and credit score simply didn't add up. The underwriters said that in order to buy she would have to put at least 10 percent down.

Helen was stretching to get into the property and she simply didn't have the extra cash. No way could she come up with an additional $15,000.

TRAP

Helen might have qualified for a subprime mortgage (see Chapter 6). However, that would have meant a significantly higher interest rate and possibly more closing costs.

So, Helen made the seller an offer. She would put down 5 percent. And the seller would lend her 5 percent. Then she would get a 90 percent mortgage from a lending institution.

Seller-Financed Deal

Down from buyer	5%	$ 15,000
Second mortgage from seller	5%	$ 15,000
90% mortgage from bank	<u>90%</u>	<u>$270,000</u>
	100%	$300,000

Helen still ended up with the same price for the home. And her down payment was the same. She just had two loans instead of one.

TRAP

Many lenders today are applying a "combined loan-to-value ratio, or CLTV," to their first mortgages. What this means is that all loans on the property cannot exceed a certain percentage. If a lender of a first mortgage had a 90 percent CLTV, the type of financing shown above would not work because it would require the buyer to put 10 percent *cash* down. If you need to work with a seller's second mortgage, be sure the lender of the first does not use CLTV.

TIP

Many lenders of first mortgages have specific rules regarding second mortgages. If they will allow you to use a second mortgage for a portion of the down payment, they may require that the second mortgage must be for a term of at least five years, although a few will allow as short a term as three years. Their reasoning is that if the second mortgage is for any shorter term, when it comes due, your house may not have appreciated sufficiently to allow you to refinance. As a consequence, the seller/lender of the second mortgage might foreclose, which could threaten the stability of the first.

Will Sellers Cooperate?

Some will cooperate, some won't. You can only ask. In some cases, sellers will agree, but with conditions. Some will not want to give you a long-term second mortgage. They may insist on a shorter 18-month or two-year second. When you point out that this will preclude you from getting a first, they may recommend a "trick" second or a "silent" second.

A trick second is where the sales agreement shows a three- to five-year second mortgage. But you and the seller agree that you will have a shorter term, and when all the documents are recorded, you record a shorter second mortgage than the agreement calls for. This depends on the lender of the first mortgage not seeing all of the documents recorded. These days, however, lenders have wised up to this trick and normally demand to see all documents.

Some buyers, in response, have come up with a silent second. This is where you record the three- to five-year second mortgage, as agreed. Then, a month or so after the transaction, you and the seller record a new second mortgage for a shorter term or sign a separate agreement to pay off the second mortgage earlier. Again, you have subverted the rules of the lender of the first mortgage.

TRAP

Beware of either the trick or the silent second. True, you may get away with using such a subterfuge because the lender of the first simply won't know what's happened. But, if you ever get into trouble and go into foreclosure, particularly during the early years of ownership, everything will come to light and the holder of the first mortgage, besides foreclosing on the property, may charge you with fraud. Facing fraud means that you could be liable both civilly and criminally and that you could be forced to defend yourself against the federal government. (Most lenders of first mortgages are protected against fraud by federal law.)

While getting a seller to take back a longer second mortgage may be difficult, it could be a whole lot easier than the trouble you could get into from a trick or silent second.

Can Creative Financing Cut My Monthly Payment?

Another use of creative financing is to help you reduce your monthly payments. This can be an extremely helpful means of financing a home, but only in a soft market. The way it works is simple. As a condition of sale, you get the seller to give you a mortgage with no interest and no monthly payments. (The principal is all due in a single balloon payment a few years down the road.)

Of course, no seller will accept a no interest/no monthly payment second mortgage in a strong market. There's no reason to, unless you sweeten the pot, which usually means offering a higher price. Good buyers will be coming in with cash.

However, this plan may fly without a higher price in a weak market when there simply aren't any buyers around. In order to get any sale at all, a seller may consider it.

TIP

Look for a seller who doesn't need all the cash out of a property in order to move on to another. If the seller needs cash, the deal can't be made no matter how you butter it up. Remember that most sellers are selling only to buy again somewhere else.

I have seen no interest/no monthly payments second mortgages written fairly frequently in a cold market. Often it may be the only way the seller is going to be able to sell the property, and for that reason, it may be acceptable. In a hot market, they are almost impossible to find.

Can Creative Financing Cut My Costs and Red Tape?

There is one additional advantage of having the seller carry back the mortgage: The seller normally will not charge any fees for the service. It would be a rare seller indeed who charged points, for example, for a carry-back second mortgage—or who charged processing or document fees, something that institutional lenders charge all the time. When you have the seller finance the sale, amongst other things, it also means that the financing is a lot cheaper for you.

What Is a Wraparound?

Thus far, we've been assuming that the seller would be willing to give you a second mortgage when you offer to buy his or her property.

However, some sellers are quite wary. They are concerned about your ability and desire to repay the mortgage. For example, what if the seller gives you a big second mortgage and then you don't make the payments on the first?

This puts the seller in a difficult position. To protect himself or herself, once the seller learns about the default, he or she must foreclose upon you, all the while fending off the institutional lender of the first.

Many sellers who would otherwise be willing to help buyers with financing won't do it because of their fear of the buyer not living up to the obligations on the first mortgage, thereby forcing them into a difficult foreclosure. The wraparound, or "all-inclusive second mortgage," is one solution to this problem.

TIP

The wraparound, or wrap, blends two mortgages, typically one with a high interest rate and one with a low rate. This provides the lender with a higher yield than just the low rate. Because of this, the lender can sometimes offer the borrower a lower blended interest rate than might otherwise be available. Thus, a wrap can benefit both borrower and lender.

The wrap has been used for years in commercial financing of real estate. It gained popularity in residential property in the mid-1970s as a way of getting around "due-on-sale clauses" (preventing assumptions), thus allowing buyers to assume sellers' existing low interest rate mortgages.

It fell out of vogue in real estate when the due-on-sale clause in existing mortgages was widely upheld in precedent-setting court cases. However, any time the real estate market dips downward and sellers look for new and creative ways of helping buyers purchase their homes, it comes back into vogue.

How Does a Wrap Work?

In its simplest form, the seller gives you a single mortgage that includes a new second as well as an old, assumable first. However, instead of making two mortgage payments, you make one—to the seller. The seller then makes the payment on the existing first mortgage and keeps the difference, which is the payment on the second.

Notice the difference here between a wrap and a traditional second. In the traditional second, you are the borrower of record on both the first and the second mortgages and make two payments, one on each mortgage. In the wrap you are the borrower of record on only one mortgage, the wraparound. The seller then forwards your payments to the lender of the first.

TRAP

You can get in trouble trying to wrap around an existing *nonassumable* first mortgage. The reason is simple. As soon as the sale is recorded, it gives the lender of the first mortgage constructive notice that the property has changed hands. Foreclosure could result.

If a lender discovers that you've wrapped around a nonassumable first mortgage, it can exert the due-on-sale clause, found in virtually all nonassumable mortgages, and call in the loan. (Remember, *nonassumable* means that as soon as the property is sold, the mortgage must be paid off. Putting the wrap on the property, in effect, results in the first mortgage becoming immediately due and payable.)

In actual practice, according to lenders with whom I've talked, most discover the wrap less than 50 percent of the time. And those that do discover it frequently overlook the problem if their loan is current and paid on time. Their philosophy is that they'd rather keep a good, paying borrower than get into the hassle of a foreclosure. Nevertheless, it's not something to risk the price of an entire home on.

What Are the Ideal Conditions for a Wrap?

In order for a wrap to work, the first mortgage must either be new or, if it's existing, must be assumable. (FHA and VA loans are often assumable, and it may be possible to wrap them in this fashion.)

In the case of a new mortgage, often both the seller and the buyer are named in the mortgage. In the event the borrower doesn't make payments, this allows the seller the right to make payments on the first mortgage and keep it current while foreclosing on the wrap.

In the case of an assumable mortgage, such as an FHA-insured or VA-guaranteed loan (which are not all assumable any more; you must verify this, first), often no notice of the wrap need be given to the lender. The new wrap loan is simply placed on the property, and the seller continues making payments on the existing first.

What If the Seller Wants to Wrap a Nonassumable?

Sometimes a seller will want to wrap around a nonassumable first mortgage in spite of the problems. You, the buyer, may be told that to avoid accelerating the mortgage because of the due-on-sale clause, the title won't actually be transferred to you. Rather, it will be held in escrow or will be in some other form, until you can pay off the equivalent of the second-mortgage portion of the wrap. Then the seller will transfer, and you can get a new first mortgage.

Remember, the problem here is caused by the fact that the existing mortgage cannot be assumed. The wrap, in this case, is a ploy to get around the nonassumption problem.

Beware of this kind of a deal, as it may end up costing you a lot of money as well as the house. In real estate, your interest in the property is evidenced by title, which means a recorded deed in your name. If you don't have a recorded title, you don't effectively own the property. Without your knowledge, the seller, conceivably, could refinance it or even sell it to someone else! Without title, you aren't properly protected.

In a nonrecorded wrap, the best you are likely to have is a contract with the seller. However, no matter how ironclad the contract may appear to be, your only recourse in the event the seller fails to live up to the terms may be to take the seller to court—a long, arduous, and costly process with unpredictable results.

What to Include When You Ask for Seller Financing

It's important to understand that everything in real estate is negotiable. That includes the second mortgage that you seek from the seller. What this means for you is that you can plan the terms and conditions of the loan so that they give you, the borrower, the greatest advantage. This is not to say that the seller will accept your terms. However, unless you have terms you want, how will you know? The following are some terms to look for.

Lower Interest Rate

Of course, one of the most important items to consider is the interest rate. As with most things, this is a trade-off. The higher the interest rate, the more likely the seller is to accept this kind of financing. The lower the interest rate, the less likely. In other words, the more interest you are willing to pay the seller on this note, the more desirable it is.

TIP

The trade-off is usually between purchase price and interest rate. If you are offering a good purchase price (close to market or what the seller is asking), you are more likely to get a low interest rate. On the other hand, if you are lowballing the seller, demanding a low price, you are better off offering a higher and more appealing interest rate on the second.

TRAP

Be aware of usury laws. Some states still have laws that limit the amount of interest that a seller can charge on a second mortgage. Any amount over that rate is considered usurious and unlawful. (These same laws may not apply to first mortgages offered by institutions.) The seller may insist on an interest rate that is above the usury rate for your state. You can then inform the seller of the problem and in this way get a lower interest rate on your mortgage than you might otherwise secure.

Note: Some states specifically exempt seller financing from usury laws. Here, as a seller, you can charge any amount of interest you want.

Longer Payoff Period

Another negotiable item is the length of the mortgage. A second (or a wrap) can be for any length of time. It can be for three months, three years, or 30 years. It's all up to what you and the seller agree upon.

In most cases, the longer the term, the better for you, the borrower. Most sellers want second mortgages for a relatively short time, 18 months to two years. Often during that time you pay interest only, which means at the end, you still owe the full amount that you borrowed—a balloon payment.

As a result, you must usually refinance or sell the home before the term of the seller's financing runs out. Naturally, the longer the second, therefore, the better it usually is for you.

On the other hand, sellers usually, but not always, want their money out quickly. Thus, the shorter the term, the more appealing the second is likely to be. Again, if you ask for a longer second mortgage, be prepared to give someplace else, such as offering a higher interest rate or perhaps a higher price. On the other hand, if you're willing to settle for a short-term second, say one year, you may be able to negotiate for a lower interest rate (or no interest) and a lower purchase price.

TIP

Most sellers want their money as soon as possible so that they can put it into another home. But sometimes a seller has different ideas. Sellers who are retiring or who have other assets often want a long-term mortgage at a good rate so that they can collect interest, which is usually better than they can get at the bank. Find out your seller's motivation. If, indeed, the seller is looking for interest income, a long-term second mortgage may be to both parties' advantage.

TRAP

Beware of short-term seconds. You can never know what the market will be like three or two years or six months into the future. You may say to yourself, "Sure, it'll be a cinch to refinance when the short-term second comes due." But by then interest rates may take a jump up and you won't be able to refinance. Or you could be laid off and not have the income to qualify for a new mortgage. Or the market may head into a tailspin and you may not be able to sell. Always allow yourself as much of an escape route as possible. In terms of seconds, this means get enough time for you to ride out most adversities. To my mind, any second for less than five years is risky.

Many institutional lenders today are giving long-term (15-year or more) seconds at competitive interest rates. If there is a problem with seller financing, see if a lending institution can help out.

Better Conditions

Finally, there are the conditions of the second. Keep in mind that whatever conditions are imposed in the second are strictly a matter of negotiation between you and the seller. Unlike a first mortgage from an institutional lender, where the conditions will be dictated to you, in a creative second almost everything is negotiable.

In most cases, buyer and seller will simply fill out a "standard" second-mortgage agreement that a title insurance, escrow company, or broker will provide. However, you can easily deviate from the printed text. Be sure you have a good real estate attorney working with you.

Late Payment Penalty.   One matter you will want to consider is that of late payment. In almost all first mortgages, there is a provision that if your payment is more than two weeks late, you will be fined a penalty often equal to 5 percent of the mortgage payment ($50 on a $1,000 payment).

This clause does not have to be inserted into the second. Unless the seller insists upon it, it would be to the buyer's advantage, in fact, to have it left out.

TIP

Some states have a limit on the amount of a late payment penalty. Also, the penalty may or may not be applicable to a balloon payment in your state. Check with a local attorney for help negotiating better terms.

The penalty for late payment can be a negotiating point. If the seller intends to sell the second to an investor, it is vital to have the penalty. Most investors will either not buy or pay less for a second without a penalty clause. Therefore, if the seller insists on a penalty clause in the second, you may argue for a better term or interest rate.

Subordination Clause.   This is a clause that you may very well want to have in the second, but which the seller, if he or she is bright at all, will usually frown upon. It is difficult to get sellers to agree to subordinate, but if you can, it can be a real plus to you.

A subordination clause means that the second mortgage remains in place even if you refinance the first. While this may seem obvious, it is not. To understand why, it is necessary to remember how mortgages are placed on real estate. They flow chronologically in the order in which they were recorded. What makes a first a first is not so much anything that is stated in the paperwork but the fact that it was recorded first, before any other mortgages. A second was recorded second, a third was recorded third, and so on.

Let's say you have a first and a second and you want to refinance the first. In order to do this, you have to pay off the existing first and get a new mortgage. However, as soon as you pay off the existing first, the existing second moves up and becomes "first" in chronological order. Therefore, you could not refinance the old first mortgage with a new first mortgage until you also paid off the second.

The solution is the subordination clause. When put into a second it requires that mortgage to hold its place. The second remains a second regardless of what happens to the first. If you pay off the first, you can then refinance and get a brand-new first *and the second holds its position*.

The importance to you of this is the fact that you can usually get a first mortgage for a lower interest rate, longer term, and higher amount than a second. Also, by keeping the second in its position, you can refinance, get more money out, and not have to pay off the second. This latter reason, of course, is why sellers don't like it. A subordination clause weakens a second.

TIP

A seller might be induced into taking a subordination clause if you limit it. For example, you could insert a clause saying that you will get a first of no more than a certain amount. Or you can subordinate only one time. Limiting the amount of the first protects the seller's second.

Automatic Refinance Clause.   This is a tricky little clause that could be worth its weight in gold. The refinance clause simply states that when the second comes due, the seller agrees to refinance it. In other words, your second mortgage may be for three years. At the end of the three years, at your (the borrower's) option, it can automatically be refinanced for an additional three years.

Why would the seller accept such a condition? Usually the clause states that the refinance will be at or slightly above then-current mortgage market rate for first mortgages. In other words, if at the end of three years (in this case) the market rate for conventional first mortgages is 8 percent, the second will be refinanced at, say, 9 percent. If the seller doesn't need the cash, this is an excellent way to lock in money for an additional period of time.

If you get a refinance clause inserted into your second, be sure that it is tied to a standard index, which can be provided by any lender (see Chapter 23).

TIP

If you're daring, you may agree to a very high interest rate on the refinance option, say 5 percent above going mortgage market rates. The seller may think that he or she is getting a real bonus here, which you can use as a negotiating tool elsewhere in the deal. In reality, of course, the seller is getting nothing, since the refinance is at your option. You can choose not to exercise it and instead to refinance elsewhere or sell the property.

Size of Second Relative to Down.   While it's true that everything is negotiable, some things are harder to negotiate than others. For example, it may be to your advantage to offer a 5 percent down payment and a 15 percent second. However, if the seller wants to dispose of that second, he or she will find it difficult to do so if you only put 5 percent down. In order for a second to be marketable to an investor, the buyer must typically put at least 10 percent down.

Will a Seller Give Me a First Mortgage?

Thus far we've been discussing sellers who are willing to give part of the equity to you in the form of a second mortgage. But there's another, though much smaller, class of sellers who are willing to make first mortgages.

These sellers are typically older people who have been in the property for 20 to 30 years and have either paid off or almost paid off their existing mortgage(s). These people may not have any use for a large amount of cash, as they would receive in an all-cash sale. But instead they may be interested in a kind of annuity. They want so much each month on which to live. A first mortgage is an ideal answer for them—and for you as well.

Besides, if the seller carries the first, you may get the mortgage for slightly below market interest rates. But, you probably won't have to pay points or other loan fees. And you may not have to qualify as strictly as you would for an institutional lender. A seller may accept a borrower with slightly blemished credit, with a lower down payment, even with less income (less ability to repay) than an institutional lender would, simply to get the house sold and to get an income-producing mortgage.

TIP

To my mind, it is worth paying more for a property where the seller will carry the first. The benefits in quicker and easier qualifying as well as lower costs more than justify a higher price.

Contract of Sale

A final mortgage device we'll discuss is a "land contract of sale." This is a dangerous tool for the unwary.

Here, instead of actually selling you the property with a deed, the seller gives you a contract to purchase. (It's called a "land contract," because years ago that's how land was frequently bought and sold.) You give the seller some money as a down payment and then make monthly payments. Traditionally, you made payments until you paid off the property. Then the seller recorded a deed in your favor and the property was yours.

Today, the time period is often three to five years and what you're doing is paying the seller enough for a down payment. When you've paid that amount, you go out and get a mortgage and the seller gives you the deed.

The contract of sale is a useful tool when the buyer doesn't have the down payment and other more conventional types of financing are not available. What should be apparent, however, is the opportunity for abuse. The buyer does not own the property but only has a contract. Therefore, if something goes wrong, the buyer's only recourse is through the court system, often a long, tedious, and expensive process.

What could go wrong? The seller could sell the same property under a contract of sale twice—or 10 times. The seller could refuse to record the deed in favor of the buyer even after the contract terms were met. The contract itself might be incorrectly drawn, resulting in the buyer not being able to claim the property.

TRAP

Don't use a contract of sale unless you have a very good attorney draw it up and approve it for you.

To help protect a buyer who uses a contract of sale, some counties now allow the recording of the contract even if it has only the buyer's signature. (Normally, all signatures are required for recording.) Having the contract recorded puts a "cloud" on the title and helps prevent the seller from selling it out from under the buyer to a third party.

How Do I Negotiate with the Seller?

We've discussed a variety of options that you may want to consider when having the seller help with the financing. One last matter needs to be discussed: the actual negotiation process. How do you negotiate with the seller to get what you want?

There's a three-step process that I use that may be helpful to you:

Step One.   Identify what you want.
Step Two.   Give in order to get.
Step Three.   Try to be flexible.

The bottom line is to remember that everything in real estate is negotiable, including terms. Many sellers simply can't or won't consider helping with the financing. But, it usually won't hurt to ask in terms of an offer. (It can hurt if you make an offer asking for favorable terms and lose out to another buyer who comes in with all cash.)

The real trick is getting the right balance between terms, price, and mortgage amount.

16

Should I Consider an FHA or a VA Mortgage?

During the 1950s and part of the 1960s, some of the most popular mortgages in real estate were those offered under the Federal Housing Authority (FHA) and the Veterans Administration (VA) programs. In those days, it seemed that when a buyer bought a home, he or she first tried to get one of these mortgages. Only after this proved impossible would the buyer settle for a "conventional," or nongovernment, mortgage.

During the 1970s, however, particularly when housing prices sky-rocketed, the allure of these mortgages diminished. Private mort-gage insurance (PMI) was available to provide low down payment conventional financing. Additionally, the bureaucratic red tape made FHAs and VAs less desirable choices. By the end of the 1970s, fewer than 10 percent of all mortgages were from these government programs.

Then in the 1980s the FHAs and VAs came roaring back. Assum-ability became important, and these loans were all assumable. Recently, FHA loans have again fallen into disfavor, largely because of relatively low maximum mortgage amounts. However, new legislation that raises the maximum may be enacted by the time you read this.

FHA Mortgages

The FHA does not usually lend money to borrowers. Under the most commonly used programs, the FHA isn't even in the mortgage lending business. Instead, it insures mortgages. The borrower gets a loan from a lender, for instance, a bank. If it's an FHA loan, the government insures payment of the mortgage to the lender. If the borrower doesn't make the payments, the FHA steps in and pays off the lender. With an FHA loan, the lender can't lose.

There are a number of FHA programs. They have included the following:

Title II

203(b)	Financing of one- to four-family dwellings
203(b)	Special financing for veterans
207	Financing rental housing and mobile home parks
221(d)	Financing low-cost one- to four-family dwellings for displaced or moderate-income families
222	Financing one-family homes for service personnel
234(f)	Financing condominium units
234(d)	Financing condominium projects and condominium conversion projects
235	Assisting low-income families to make home purchase by subsidizing mortgage interest payments

Title I

(b)	Financing purchase of a mobile home unit

Many of these programs have been cut or at least severely pruned as federal budget cutting has proceeded in Washington. But the basic program, 203(b), still helps finance home mortgages.

Advantages of FHA Mortgages

There are many advantages to the FHA mortgage. These include the following:

1. *They may be assumable.* At one time, all FHA loans were fully assumable by any buyer. That meant that any time you wanted

to sell your property, all you had to do was turn your existing (often low interest) FHA loan over to the buyer. After 1987, however, the FHA imposed stricter rules. Now buyers must qualify, including credit reports and income verifications. When the buyer does qualify, however, he or she still can (in some cases) take over the existing interest rate mortgage. Additionally, the seller may continue to be liable under certain circumstances. For mortgages issued after December 1986, liability may extend for five years. For those issued after December 1989, liability may extend for 10 years or more.

2. *There are no prepayment penalties.* An FHA mortgage may be paid off in full at any time without penalty.

3. *Not only does the buyer have to qualify for the FHA mortgage, but the property has to qualify as well.* This means something more than the house simply being appraised for enough money to warrant the mortgage. It means that the house has to qualify structurally. Sometimes on FHA mortgages, the seller will be required to bring any substandard construction up to current building codes. Any damage, such as that done by wind, water, termites, fungus, erosion, and so forth, might also have to be corrected. When a buyer purchases a home under an FHA program, he or she has virtually a government stamp of approval on it.

Disadvantages of FHA Mortgages

There are some disadvantages (not many) to the FHA mortgage. These include the following:

1. *The maximum loan amount is relatively low.* That's all right for some parts of the country. But for the West Coast, East Coast, and areas in between where residential property prices are high, the maximum is frequently just too low for the FHA to be a useful source of financing.

2. *The borrower must occupy the property to get the low down payment.* If you want to pay 3 percent down, then you must be an owner–occupant. You can still get the FHA financing as a nonoccupant investor, *but* you're required to put 15 percent down.

3. *The borrower must pay a mortgage insurance premium.* The premium is a substantial amount.

Mortgage Premium

The mortgage insurance premium (MIP) for residential property must be paid up front at the time the loan is made. (In the past, it would have been paid monthly as a slight increase in payment.) The percentage used for the mortgage premium has frequently changed.

Down Payment

As noted, the down payment for FHA mortgages is 3 percent or less for owner-occupied property or 15 percent for investor-purchased property. In the past, this down payment had to be in cash. Recently, however, the FHA has allowed it to be handled through secondary financing. It works like this: If you want to buy a piece of property using an FHA mortgage, you can either put 15 percent cash down *or* you can put up a second mortgage *on a different piece of property*. Note that the second mortgage *cannot be on the property being financed*. Rather, it has to be on some other property. For example, you may own a lot or another house. You can give the seller of the property you are currently buying a second mortgage on your other house. The FHA is part of the Department of Housing and Urban Development, or HUD, with offices in all major cities and main offices in Washington, D.C.

VA Mortgages

The VA program is similar to the FHA program in that it is administered by the government. However, that's where the similarities tend to end. For new VA mortgages, the borrower has to have one vital ingredient: He or she has to be a veteran and have qualifying duty.

The biggest advantage the VA loan program has over the FHA is that in many cases there is *no down payment*. The borrower doesn't have to put up anything to make the purchase (with, of course, the exception of closing costs). Literally millions of veterans have used the VA program. Some have gone back and used it many times. (Soon we'll see how.)

How the VA Program Works

Like an FHA mortgage, the VA loan is obtained from a lender such as a bank or an S&L. However, while the FHA insures the lender against loss, the VA "guarantees" a portion of the loan (actually, the first money likely to be lost by the lender). If the veteran defaults, the VA will pay the first 25 percent of the debt. Since that usually represents any loss a lender is likely to sustain, it virtually removes the lender from any risk. In actual practice, when a borrower defaults, the VA, like the FHA, buys the entire mortgage back from the lender and then tries to resell the property. (These are called "VA repos" or "FHA repos.") Unlike the FHA, however, the VA, if it sustains any loss on the resale of the property, can come after the borrower, a veteran, to try to recoup its loss.

Down Payment

There is no official maximum VA mortgage, although lenders generally will not loan more than a maximum of $240,000. The down payment is negotiated between the lender and the veteran. The VA charges a funding fee to the veteran, depending on the amount put down. The fee schedule is as follows:

Less than 5% down	2.0 (% of loan balance)
5% to 10% down	1.5
Over 10% down	1.25

The funding fee is paid by the veteran to the VA. Points are paid by the seller.

Entitlement

The portion that the VA guarantees is called the veteran's "entitlement." When the program was first started, the entitlement was only $2,000. However, housing prices have gone up, and so has the entitlement. Recently it was a maximum of $60,000 for some loans over $144,000.

Reusing Entitlement.   The veteran's entitlement usually remains with the vet for life. This means that if the veteran sells the property and the VA loan is paid off, he or she may reapply for and receive back the entitlement; he or she would then be able to get another VA loan.

Using Remaining Entitlement.   Because the entitlement amount has risen, there are many veterans who bought homes years ago when the entitlement was lower and who still are eligible for a portion of their entitlement. For example, if a vet bought a home in the 1950s, when the entitlement was $5,000, he or she may today be able to claim the difference between the entitlement used ($5,000) and the current maximum.

Qualifying for a VA Loan

Unlike the FHA or even conventional lenders, the VA does not have a hard-and-fast formula that it uses to qualify a veteran. Rather, it has criteria. The criteria are as follows:

1. A history of good credit
2. Sufficient income to make the payments and support the veteran's family
3. An eligible veteran with available entitlement

The VA has been extremely flexible in the past regarding mortgages to vets. I have seen cases where a vet who was turned down by the lender went directly to the VA and won a reversal on the strength of a promise to make payments. A large part of the VA program has been aimed at helping veterans get a home and get started.

Eligibility Requirements

The eligibility requirements for VA loans always seem to be changing. To determine what the current requirements are, you should check with your nearest VA office. Or check the VA's home loan guarantee program at www.homeloans.va.gov.

VA Appraisals

When a veteran applies for a mortgage, the VA appraises the property and then issues a Certificate of Reasonable Value (CRV). Sales contracts that specify that the borrower is obtaining a VA loan must also specify that if the property does not appraise for the sale price (the CRV doesn't equal the sale price), the veteran may withdraw from the sale, *or,* the veteran may opt to pay more than the CRV. However, the loan amount will still be based on the CRV, not the final sale price.

Automatics

Because of the long delays that have occurred in the past in funding VA loans, the VA has designated certain lenders to handle automatic funding. What this means is that the lender qualifies the veteran, makes the loan, and closes the deal. Then the lender secures the loan guarantee from the VA. Most large S&Ls, banks, and mortgage bankers are approved for automatics.

Owner-Occupancy Requirement

The VA has long required that the veteran plan to occupy the property. If the property is larger than a home (a duplex, for example), the vet must plan to occupy one unit on the property. There are no age requirements for either VA or FHA loans.

Impound Accounts

Both VA and FHA mortgages require the borrower to establish an "impound account" (also called a "trust fund account"). This simply means that the borrower must pay for the taxes and insurance on the property on a monthly basis (that is, the borrower must pay $\frac{1}{12}$ of the yearly total each month). The monthly payment goes into a lender's special impound account, and the lender pays the fees at the appropriate times each year.

Maximum Loan Amounts

With FHA loans, the maximum loan amount will vary depending on the area of the country and whether the property is rural or metropolitan. As of this writing the maximum amount of the mortgage in the continental United States is around $312,000. To find out the maximum FHA loan in your area as well as more information on the FHA, go to:

www.hud.gov/buying

The maximum VA loan as of this writing is $240,000. For more information on VA loans check out:

www.homeloans.va.gov/

17

What's the Advantage of an Early Payoff?

If you're a high-income earner, the last thing you might want to do is to pay off your mortgage. You have plenty of income coming in to service the mortgage. The income tax deduction you get for mortgage interest provides you with what might possibly be your biggest tax deduction. And money in the bank that you would otherwise use to pay off the mortgage might be better spent on high-yielding investments. Paying it off might make no sense at all.

On the other hand, if you're retired and have a very small income but have a fair amount of cash in the bank, paying off that mortgage and eliminating a burdensome payment might make perfectly good sense. In this chapter we're going to consider some of the ramifications of paying off your mortgage early.

Can You Pay It Off?

Most people who can afford to pay off the mortgage on their home are more mature. Perhaps they've retired and have received a large lump-sum retirement. Or perhaps other investments have paid off handsomely and now their bank account is fat. If you're in a position to pay off your mortgage early, you are indeed unusual.

183

Additionally, there's also the matter of the mortgage itself. New mortgages tend to be high value. On the other hand, a mortgage that's been on a property for 20 years or more may already be paid way down. Now only a fraction of its original value remains.

TRAP

The decision to pay off an existing mortgage should not be taken lightly, particularly if you are retired and living on a fixed income. Don't simply rely on the information in this chapter. Consult with a trusted advisor who can analyze your particular situation. You don't want to make a mistake and put your future into jeopardy.

Should I Consider Equity Return?

I've mentioned it before, but it's particularly applicable here. The return of equity from a mortgage is much greater in its later years than in its earlier ones. When your mortgage gets to its final years, most of each monthly payment goes to principal, less and less to interest. Thus, what you are doing in those last years is rapidly paying off the mortgage and rapidly adding to your equity in the property. If you refinance to a new mortgage, even for the same amount, the majority of the payment will now go to interest.

TRAP

In the latter years of a loan, as more of the payment goes to principal, the amount of tax deduction that you get from interest declines. This can be a serious problem if you're counting on the tax deduction from the mortgage to offset income.

Many people feel that the period of rapid equity return is the golden period of the mortgage. Nevertheless, the question must be asked, could you make better use of that money that you are paying out each month? For example, let's say your monthly payments on the mortgage are $750 a month, of which $500 is going to equity and

$250 is going to interest. For practical purposes you can think of the $500 as "money in the bank." It's going toward your equity or your savings in the home.

But can you afford the $750 payment? Perhaps you are struggling to make other payments. Or perhaps you are on a fixed income. If so, and if you have significant savings, might it not be better to pay off that mortgage and avoid having to pay out $750 a month?

Oftentimes people who find themselves in the position described above have some savings in the bank that are simply not making them much money. They may only be getting 2 percent or so on those savings. They ask themselves, wouldn't it be better to take out those savings and pay off the mortgage, thus avoiding that big monthly payment?

How Do I Make the Payoff Decision?

Having a home paid off sometimes makes the difference in whether you are able to live on a low fixed income or not. With the house payment, there isn't enough interest to make it all work each month. Eliminate that house payment and the limited income might be more than enough. That's why many seniors opt to pay off their home.

Another concern, noted above, is the interest you're receiving on your money in the bank. If the interest rate on the mortgage is *higher* than the interest rate on the money in savings, it may make economic sense to pay off the loan.

Consider this: Let's say the outstanding balance on the mortgage is $50,000 and the interest rate is 6 percent. That means that the current year you are spending roughly $3,000 in interest on that mortgage. On the other hand, let's say that you have $50,000 in the bank earning 2 percent interest. Your money that year earns $1,000.

Comparison of Mortgage with Savings

Mortgage interest paid out	– $3,000
Savings interest earned	+ $1,000
Net Loss	$2,000

The result of keeping $50,000 in the bank at a low interest rate and paying off a $50,000 mortgage at a higher rate is a loss to you of

$2,000. In short, simply by paying off the mortgage, you can pick up an additional $2,000 a year otherwise lost in interest payments.

Of course, the amount to be gained will vary according to the amount of the mortgage and the difference in interest rates. However, I think the point should be clear. Economically speaking, without any other considerations, it may make sense in this situation to pay off the mortgage.

There are, however, other considerations.

What about Tax Savings?

Generally speaking, you pay taxes on interest you receive from a savings account. (If you have the money invested in certain tax-free mutual bonds or funds, that may not be the case.) On the other hand, generally speaking you can deduct the interest you pay on your home mortgage.

Thus, if you take the money out of savings, you'll reduce the interest you receive and pay taxes on. At the same time, however, you'll also pay off the mortgage and eliminate the interest deduction there. You'll have to balance the two factors to see whether it makes sense to pay off that mortgage. Keep in mind, as noted earlier, the amount of the payment that goes to interest may be very small; hence, you may not be getting a big tax deduction for it.

TIP

Many people in lower-income brackets don't itemize on their returns. If you don't itemize, then you can't claim the interest deduction on your mortgage and it's worth nothing to you. You must still, however, pay taxes on the income received from savings.

The Problem with Real Estate Is Lack of Liquidity

There's another consideration that's well worth making, particularly for those on limited incomes. How important is it to you to have cash in the bank? If you need a cash reserve to pay for medical or other emergencies, then you may be placing yourself in jeopardy by paying off your mortgage early. You may, in fact, be jumping from the frying pan into the fire. The reason is that it's easy to get hold of cash in a savings account. Just go to the bank and withdraw it. It's hard to get hold of cash from equity in your home. You have to refinance or sell, and if it's at a time when you don't have a strong income and good credit or if the market's soft, you could have a problem.

TIP

One alternative to liquefying your home investment is to establish a revolving line of credit based on the equity in your home. You take out as much as you need and repay whenever convenient. You're only charged interest on the amount borrowed. These types of loans go by various names, the most common being "home equity loans." Almost any lender can set one up for you.

What's the Value of a Paid-Off Home?

While having cash available for living expenses and emergencies is important, there's a great deal to be said for the value of a paid-off property. I can't think of anything else in our modern world that can give one such a sense of security. You know that no matter what happens you have a place to go that a lender can't take away from you (for failing to make payments).

You have to balance the need for cash with the comfort of a paid-off mortgage.

18

How Do I Cancel My Private Mortgage Insurance?

Any time you put less than 20 percent down on the purchase of a property, you almost surely will be faced with private mortgage insurance (PMI). The PMI is a fee that goes toward guaranteeing a portion of the mortgage to the lender in the event that you default.

Many people resent the PMI charge, thinking of it as a garbage expense, unwarranted and unwanted. In truth, however it benefits the borrower as much as the lender. While it is the lender who is insured, it's that very insurance that allows the lender to make high LTV (loan-to-value) mortgages. Thus, when you get a 95 percent (or 100 percent) loan, it's the PMI that's permitting the lender to offer that much money.

There are two types of mortgage insurance: government and private. Government mortgage insurance is required on all FHA mortgages. These days you typically pay the premium for it all up front at the time you get the mortgage. Private mortgage insurance (PMI) is available on most other loans, provided both you and the property are of sufficiently high quality (creditwise and location-wise) to qualify. In this chapter, we'll consider only private mortgage insurance.

How Much Does It Cost?

The charge for PMI is collected by the lender and goes to the insurer. It is based on risk. Thus, it will be higher for a 95 percent loan than for a 90 percent loan. And it will be higher still for a 100 percent loan.

The charge also will depend on the amount of the loan that's insured. The lender can choose to insure the top 18 percent or the top 37 percent of the mortgage. The more of the mortgage covered, the higher the cost.

TIP

"Top" means that the coverage is from the maximum amount downward. For example, 37 percent coverage on a $100,000 loan means that in the event of default and loss, the insurer would pay to the lender the first $37,000 of the mortgage, leaving a balance of $63,000 unpaid.

The actual cost per month to you as a borrower for the PMI usually varies between a low of ¼ percent and a high of ¾ percent, although the top amount could be higher.

Must You Pay PMI for the Life of the Mortgage?

Lenders seldom stress the fact that at a certain point you may be able to get the PMI removed from your loan. Getting it removed should significantly reduce your monthly payment.

TRAP

You can only get the charge removed if it's charged as a separate PMI fee. If it's written into the mortgage as part of the interest rate, then it cannot be removed.

The Federal Homeowners Protection Act of 1998 dealt with the issue of removing PMI. Basically, it mandates that the PMI automatically be canceled whenever the balance of your loan drops to 78 percent of the value of the property at the time the loan was made. In other words, if you bought a $200,000 property with a 90 percent loan ($180,000), that mortgage would have to drop to $156,000 for the PMI to automatically cancel out. In terms of actual time, that's something like seven to nine years after you get the mortgage.

TIP

To qualify for automatic PMI cancellation, you must have a record of on-time loan payments.

The problem is that most homeowners don't want to wait that long. This is particularly the case in recent years where home prices have escalated upward. In some cases the value of the home has gone up within six months to the point where the mortgage is far below 80 percent of the *current* (not original) value.

How Do I Get the PMI Removed If My House Has Appreciated in Value?

The same federal Homeowners Protection Act provides a procedure for petitioning the lender to have the PMI removed earlier. There are, however, certain conditions.

Conditions for Requesting Early PMI Removal

- Your equity must equal at least 20 percent of the current value of the property (25 percent if it's a Fannie Mae or Freddie Mac mortgage).
- You must pay for an appraisal by an appraiser designated by your lender, and that appraisal must verify your equity. (If the appraisal comes in low, the lender doesn't have to remove the PMI and you're out the cost of the appraisal.)
- You must demonstrate a history of on-time payments for at least one year.
- At least two years must have elapsed since you obtained the mortgage. (You can't easily have the PMI removed in the first two years of the loan.)

TRAP

Don't expect lenders to initiate removal of the PMI no matter how much your house appreciates or how much of the mortgage you pay down. They have no incentive to do so and, at best, it just means extra accounting for them. That means that you must get the ball rolling.

Many of the problems with PMI arise out of the fact that lenders sometimes forget to tell borrowers that they may get the PMI removed after a certain time period and after their equity increases. Rather, the lenders simply keep collecting the money as long as the borrower pays it and doesn't complain.

TRAP

Make sure that payments stop when the PMI is canceled. In a very few cases, lenders apparently have removed the PMI coverage from the loan but continued to collect and pocket the fees from the borrower!

Is There Any More Government Help Coming?

There are a number of efforts in Congress to allow borrowers to deduct the PMI costs in the same way as they deduct interest. However, these have not passed as of this writing.

In all fairness to lenders and private mortgage insurers, it must be pointed out that a falling market, as was the case in the mid-1990s, meant that it was hazardous to remove the PMI. While the mortgage value could indeed be 80 percent or below, if the price of the property fell, it could rise to more than 80 percent. Keeping PMI on in that kind of market made good sense from the lender's perspective.

In up markets, leaving PMI on a property any longer than necessary makes no sense at all to the borrower. If your equity is at 20 percent or more and you have PMI, you should certainly investigate the possibility of having it removed. Contact your lender about its procedure for doing so.

19

First-Time Home Buyer and Other Special Programs

You may be eligible for special mortgage terms if you are a first-time home buyer, are a low-income family, are in a "disaster area," or have some other special need. This could help you get a mortgage and buy a house.

Today there are many mortgages specially designed for people who have special problems. Sometimes these mortgages offer below-market interest rates or reduced costs and points. If you qualify, you would be foolish not to look for and attempt to get one of them.

What If I'm a First-Time Home Buyer?

What is a first-time home buyer? If you answer that it's a person who's never bought a home before, you'd be technically incorrect. According to most government housing programs, however, a first-time home buyer is someone who has not owned a principal residence within the previous three years.

"What?" you might say. "If I previously owned three houses but have rented for three years, I qualify as a first-time home buyer?"

Maybe. But keep in mind that there are city, county, state, and federal mortgages available, and their qualifications vary enormously.

Typically, besides being a first-time home buyer, in order to qualify you must meet household size/maximum income requirements. For example, the city of Los Angeles offered a mortgage credit certificate (MCC) to certain qualifying people. While the figures change and the program is subject to change or discontinuance, as of this writing it generally offers the following:

Household size	Maximum income
1–2 people	$67,680
3 or more	$78,960

You are also limited to purchasing a new house in a targeted area up to a maximum of $431,119 or an existing house up to $369,964. (Homes in nontargeted areas have lower maximums.) Unfortunately, in high-priced areas, that tends to rule out many homes.

The MCC gives the borrower a federal income tax credit of up to 20 percent of the mortgage interest. The borrower, of course, must live in the home and keep the same mortgage. The credit reduces the taxes you pay and thus helps both in qualifying for the mortgage as well as making the payments. (For more information, check out www.lacity.org/lahd/mcc.htm.)

Other cities have similar programs.

Programs Other Than MCC

A host of different types of programs may be suited to other situations. For example, the Federal Emergency Management Agency (FEMA) coordinates low interest rate loans to victims of natural disasters. The key, however, is that the federal government must declare the area in which your home is located to be an officially designated disaster area. Most states have similar programs.

The Department of Housing and Urban Development (HUD) also offers a host of loans, some directly funded to help with financing. Through the FHA (Federal Housing Administration) there are programs designed for those with little money to put down (see Chapter 16), for farmers, and for others.

Both Fannie Mae and Freddie Mac also offer specialized programs to the first-time home buyer. In addition, there are literally hundreds of other organizations that offer special financing for those in special circumstances.

How Do I Find Out about the Various Mortgage Programs?

You'll have to do the legwork. Most of the programs are government-sponsored and that means calling, writing, and sometimes going down to government offices. Generally, you'll want to see the housing office director, but the title of the person may vary significantly.

TIP

If you're going to apply for these programs, it's a good idea to do it before contacting a lender directly. In some cases you will only be considered after you get a mortgage. In others, however, you can only be considered before you apply. Find out first and avoid being disappointed.

For FEMA, information on mortgage programs is usually widely disseminated at and around disaster sites such as earthquakes, fires, floods, and so on. You can also contact FEMA directly:

FEMA
500 C St., SW
Washington, D.C. 20472
(202) 566-1600
www.fema.gov

For HUD and FHA programs, contact the administration directly in Washington, D.C., or a state office:

HUD/FHA
451 7th St., SW
Washington, D.C. 20410
(202) 708-1112
www.hud.gov/homes/homesforsale.cfm

Also check with Fannie Mae and Freddie Mac for any programs they may be administering:

Fannie Mae
3900 Wisconsin Ave, NW
Washington, D.C. 20016-2892
202-752-7000
www.fanniemae.com

Freddie Mac
8200 Jones Beach Drive
McLean, Virginia 22101
703-903-2000
www.freddiemac.com

Finally, ask your local mortgage broker. He or she may know of programs available in your area that will be just for you.

For city and county programs, your best bet is to first contact the general information number and then ask for "housing." You'll have to work your way through to the person who handles special programs in your area. You may also want to check into my book, *How to Buy a Home When You Can't Afford It*, McGraw-Hill, 2002.

20

Reverse Equity Mortgages

The reverse equity mortgage (REM) takes money out of your home and gives it back to you on a monthly basis. It was designed to help older citizens get their equity out and still have a home to live in.

This mortgage has had a spotted past. It was first conceived on the East Coast decades ago, but only a couple of lenders tried it with mixed results. Then a few lenders in the South tried it with better results, but the savings and loan debacle of the late 1980s made it impractical to use. More recently it is seeing a comeback in different parts of the country sponsored by the FHA as the Home Equity Conversion Mortgage (HECM). (Mortgages really are an alphabet soup of letters!)

How Does a Reverse Equity Mortgage Work?

The way a basic REM works is relatively simple. It assumes that a borrower owns a house free and clear, or close to it. The lender sends out an appraiser who determines current value. Then the lender agrees to a loan-to-value ratio, typically 80 percent.

The owner/borrower can now receive 80 percent of the value. However, he or she only receives it in the form of a monthly payment, typically about as much as would be paid if the owner had borrowed the whole amount.

197

REM home equity decreases over time. As each monthly payment is made, the principal and interest on it is subtracted from the equity in the house. Thus, the mortgage amount increases.

What Happens If You Outlive the Equity in the Property?

In the past, that meant that you could be thrown out of the property! With newer plans, particularly those from the FHA, there is a provision that you get to stay in the property for your lifetime. Further, in some cases the payments continue to you regardless of how long you live.

For this reason, many lenders are very hesitant to move forward with reverse equity mortgages. However, those who have done it successfully have consulted with actuaries who come up with fairly accurate longevity tables.

TIP

The reverse equity mortgage can be a lifesaver if you have a paid-off house (or almost paid off), have little to no income, and are elderly. It can provide a steady income for your later years.

TRAP

You might not be able to give your children your home and its equity when you die if you opt for a REM. Rather, it will go to the lender.

FAQs on Reverse Equity Mortgages

How Much Money Can I Get?

Each case is different. Generally speaking, however, the older you are, the more money you'll get. The more equity you have in your home and the more it's worth, the more money you'll get.

How Big Will the Monthly Payments to Me Be?

There are several factors that determine this, and they include the following:

- Your equity in the home
- The interest rate charged
- The closing costs and other fees involved
- The kind of plan or program you choose.

Must I Own My Home?

Yes, ownership is essential, since the mortgage is based on your home ownership.

Can I Pay Back the Mortgage?

Yes, usually at any time. In the event of your death, your heirs will need to sell the home to pay back the loan.

Can I Will the Home to My Heirs?

You can only will the amount of your equity to your heirs, and that will drop each month as you receive a payment.

Can I Borrow More Than My Home's Value?

No. The total debt you incur cannot exceed the "nonrecourse limit" of the home.

Can I Refinance for More Money As My Home Appreciates?

Yes, you can, as your home increases in market value. However, you probably cannot increase the maximum limit of an existing reverse mortgage. Generally, you cannot place a second mortgage on a home that has a reverse first mortgage.

Can My Home Be Taken Away from Me?

It depends on the program, but generally speaking, no. If you top out on the amount borrowed, you may stop receiving payments. However, you will be allowed to continue living in the home. You will not be required to pay back the debt while you are alive and your heirs will not be required to pay back the debt, other than the value of the home. There will still, however, be taxes and insurance to pay.

Do I Have to Maintain My Home?

Yes, the home must be kept in reasonably good condition.

Can I Rent Out My Home?

It depends on the program. In most programs, this may trigger a requirement that the mortgage be paid back in full, immediately.

Can I Put My Son (or Daughter) on the Deed?

Changing the title in any way normally triggers an immediate demand for full repayment of the mortgage.

How Do I Find Out More?

You can contact an FHA office for information on their HECM program. They are located in most major cities, with headquarters in Washington, D.C. They can tell you if any lenders participate in the program in your area. The other two big lenders are Fannie Mae and Financial Freedom Plan. You can learn about all of these, as well as locate a lender in your state, at www.reversemortgage.org.

21

Does a New Mortgage Affect My Taxes?

There are at least three important tax considerations with regard to new mortgages:

- The deductibility of points
- The deductibility of interest
- How a mortgage affects gain or loss on sale

In this chapter we'll look into each of these topics and consider a few others besides. But before we proceed, it's important to first understand the nature of tax laws.

The tax laws are always evolving. What is true as this is written, for example, may be different by the time you read it, depending on court interpretations, IRS rulings, and new laws passed by the government. Therefore, while a serious effort has been made to see that the following material is as up to date and accurate as possible, you should not rely on it. When making any decisions involving taxation, you should first check with a competent professional such as a tax attorney or accountant.

Are Points Deductible?

Points, as you'll recall, are a form of prepaid interest that you may be required to pay to the lender in order to secure a mortgage. These are paid up front when you get the loan. The question inevitably arises, are these points deductible from your income taxes when you buy a home?

The answer is yes, generally speaking, but not usually all at once. Let's clarify. If the points represent prepaid interest, then you may deduct them. However, you must deduct them over the life of the mortgage. If the mortgage is for 30 years, then the deduction for points must be spread out over that period of time. For example, 2 points on a $120,000 mortgage for 30 years are deductible at $80 a year.

Most borrowers, however, would not find this particularly useful, since we all want deductions in the year we have the expense. How sweet it would be to be able to deduct the $5,000 we pay in points (or however much) in the year we pay it.

Can I Deduct Points in the Year I Pay Them?

There is an exception to the above rule that allows you to deduct points in the year you pay them providing you meet certain criteria. These criteria include the following:

1. *You pay the points out of your own funds.* The points are not paid out of the money loaned by the lender or in place of an appraisal fee, survey fee, attorney's fee, or similar fee.

   TIP

    Many borrowers have taken to writing a separate check to the lender to cover the cost of the points. In this way they have a paper record of having paid for them separate from funds advanced by the lender.

2. *The mortgage must be for your principal residence.* It must be used for buying or improving that residence.

TRAP

You cannot deduct points in the year paid on a mortgage for a second residence, even though interest on that mortgage may be deductible. You may be able to deduct the points over the life of the mortgage.

3. *The amount of points charged must be customary for the area.*

TRAP

If you "buy down" a mortgage (by paying additional points up front), the government may determine that the points you paid were in excess of what is customary for your area and disallow the deduction in the year paid.

4. *The points must represent interest.* They cannot be the fees paid for appraisals, credit reports, or the origination fees charged for FHA loans or special fees charged for VA loans. They must be computed as a percentage of the mortgage principal and clearly be spelled out as points on the settlement statement.

TIP

The preceding rules apply to property that is your principal residence. If you are purchasing or refinancing a rental property, different rules apply. There, you may deduct the points only over the life of the mortgage; however, you may also be able to deduct your other costs and fees as a business expense. Check with your accountant.

TRAP

Your principal residence is generally the place where you spend most of your time. Although the rules here are somewhat foggy, the government has become increasingly strict in determining what constitutes a principal residence. Unless you spend more than 50 percent of your time there, it might be hard to prove that a house was your principal residence.

5. *The deductions are applicable only if the points do not exceed the maximum interest deduction allowable on a residence.*

6. *You must use a cash method of accounting.* You have to report your income and deduct expenses in the year they occur.

Deducting points paid on a home mortgage is one of the biggest areas of confusion when it comes to paying taxes for homeowners. The good news is that if you handle it correctly, you probably can deduct some of the points. The bad news is that you probably do need a tax consultant to look at your particular situation to determine what may be deductible and what may not.

Can I Deduct Interest Paid on a Mortgage?

At one time, all the interest paid on any mortgage was fully deductible. (At one time, in fact, you could prepay interest years in advance and then deduct it in the year paid!) All that has changed, however, under the guise of tax reform. Tax reform has severely limited the amount of interest on a home mortgage that you may deduct from your taxes.

Today, the amount of interest you can deduct on a home that you own is limited. (*Note:* These rules indicated below do not apply to rental/investment property. Different rules may apply in that situation.)

1. The deduction applies only to your principal residence and to a second home. If it's a second home, you must use it part of the year.

2. The maximum mortgage amount deducted can be $1 million, provided that the mortgage was used to purchase, build, or improve your home.

TIP

Any mortgage debt taken out prior to October 13, 1987, is grandfathered in. For example, if you took out a mortgage for $3 million prior to that date, the interest on all of it is deductible. However, if you took out a mortgage after October 13, 1987, the maximum mortgage amount on which interest is deductible is $1 million, including any mortgages grandfathered in.

3. If you take out a mortgage (refinance) on your home for purposes other than to improve, build, or add on, you are limited to $100,000 of debt on which interest may be deducted.

4. Other important rules and limitations may apply, so check with your accountant.

It's important to understand how this rule works. For example, you may purchase a home with a mortgage of $150,000. Under the rule, all of the interest on this mortgage is presumably deductible. After you buy the property, you decide to add to the house and secure a mortgage for $250,000 more. If all the money is used to build or improve the property, all the interest on the second mortgage may be deductible. However, if you took out a second mortgage on the same property for $250,000 and used the money to start a business of your own, only the interest on the first $100,000 of the debt would be deductible.

TRAP

If you take out a mortgage against your home and then buy bonds that are tax-free or otherwise receive tax-free income, the interest on the mortgage may not be deductible.

TIP

There may be a special exception available if you use the money for education. Check with your accountant.

As can be seen from the preceding examples and explanations, while home interest is generally deductible, it isn't necessarily so. That being the case, you should consult with an accountant on the tax ramifications before taking out any mortgage.

What about the Tax Considerations When I Refinance?

Generally speaking, for tax purposes, the amount of financing on a home is irrelevant when it comes to capital gains taxes. In other words, it doesn't matter if you paid cash or had a 100 percent mortgage.

Let's try an example. Say that 10 years ago you purchased a home for $100,000. You obtained an $80,000 mortgage as part of the purchase price. Since that time the value of your home went up to $250,000. You decide to refinance and take out an additional $100,000 in another mortgage. Do you have any capital gains taxes to pay at the time of the refinance?

The answer is no. When you refinance, you do not increase your capital gains tax liability. But, you are reducing your equity in the property, and that could come back to haunt you later on. It is for this reason that many times people will choose to refinance instead of sell, particularly with investment properties.

TRAP

If you refinance for more than the current balance of your acquisition loan (the amount of financing you incurred when you purchased), you may be restricted in the amount of interest you can deduct annually. Further, points incurred when refinancing are not fully deductible in the current year. Check with an accountant.

What about Tax Consequences When I Sell?

Selling, however, is a different matter. If you have a capital gain on the sale, you may owe taxes on that gain. Gain is calculated as the difference between your adjusted basis and your net selling price. The actual calculation can be tricky and should be made by a tax specialist.

TRAP

If you refinanced earlier, you reduced your equity. However, when you sell, the tax is calculated on gain, not equity. So, you may be shocked to discover that you owe a significant tax bill, even though your remaining equity in the property is small. That's the hidden tax consequence of refinancing.

What about the "Up to $500,000 Exclusion"?

When you sell a principal residence in which you have lived for two out of the preceding five years, a married couple filing jointly may exclude up to $500,000 of the gain. A single person may exclude up to $250,000 of the gain. Special rules and exceptions apply, so check with your accountant.

How Does Mortgage Interest Compare to Personal Interest?

It is worthwhile noting that today all personal interest is nondeductible. That means that interest on your car loan, credit cards, department stores charges, and so forth are not deductible.

On the other hand, mortgage interest, up to certain limits, is deductible. Essentially that means that if you borrow $20,000 in personal debt, there is no tax deduction for the interest. However, if you borrow $20,000 on a home equity loan, even if the money is over and above your cost of acquiring the property (up to the $100,000 limit discussed earlier), the money may be tax deductible.

For this reason, many people today are opting for the home equity loan over other types of personal finance for their personal financing needs.

TRAP

Keep in mind that we're only talking about the deductibility of mortgages on your principal residence. Mortgages on second homes may not apply. Different rules will also apply for rental property.

TIP

Be careful of home equity mortgages that are sold on the basis of their tax deductibility. Oftentimes the "friendly" lender really doesn't closely examine your personal finances to discover whether or not such a mortgage would benefit you taxwise. It could turn out that the interest on the loan isn't tax deductible when you thought it was. That could be a rather annoying discovery later on.

What about Mortgages That Are Forgiven?

Generally speaking, mortgage debt that is forgiven is considered taxable income by the IRS. That has caused some real shock and dismay for many borrowers.

TRAP

If you're upside down (that is, you owe more than the property is worth) and get a short payoff from the lender, it means that the lender is, in essence, forgiving a portion of your mortgage. That portion may be considered income to you by the IRS. Check with a good tax attorney before accepting any short payoffs.

What about Late Payments on a Mortgage?

Late payments generally may be deductible, if they constitute interest. On the other hand, if they are for a specific service that the lender performs, such as sending out late payment notices, they probably are not deductible.

What about Interest on a Mortgage That Is Over and Above the Value of the Property?

This happens when there is negative amortization or when you get a 125 percent mortgage. Generally speaking, you can't deduct interest unless you pay it. By converting it to principal, as in negative amortization, it stops being interest. You may, however, be able to deduct the extra interest incurred because of the additional principal.

On the matter of interest paid on a mortgage over and above the value of the property, if the mortgage is in truth a personal loan (at least the part over 100 percent LTV), the interest probably is not deductible. Remember, generally you can only deduct *mortgage* interest, not interest on a personal loan. This is one of the great traps with 125 percent mortgages.

The subject of taxes and mortgages is enormous and treacherous. What appears to make good sense on the surface may have nothing at all to do with the way the tax rules are interpreted or applied. Therefore, as noted in the beginning, you are urged to consult your tax professional before you make any move involving real estate, including refinancing or purchasing with a mortgage. It may very well be that by just structuring the deal slightly differently, you can save yourself an enormous amount of taxes later on.

22

When Should I Refinance?

There are many reasons to refinance. If you have a lot of equity, you most certainly will keep thinking to yourself about all the ways you could use that money, if you could just get it out of the property (buy a boat, take a vacation, pay for education, and so on). If interest rates have dropped, you'll wonder if maybe now is the time to roll over that old higher-rate mortgage into a lower-rate one.

In this chapter we'll look at three of the refinance temptations and try to come up with a method of determining whether it's a good or bad idea for you. We'll cover the following:

- Falling interest rates
- Home improvement loans
- Debt consolidation mortgages

What If Interest Rates Are Falling?

During the first years of this century, interest rates fell to historic lows. Many people who had purchased homes earlier realized their current mortgage interest rate was higher than the rates for new loans. The question for them became, when does it pay to refinance?

211

In the old days, there was a rule of thumb that said that interest rates had to fall about 2 percent before refinancing made sense. That's because the costs of the refinancing (title insurance, escrow, mortgage points, and other fees) were so high. Thus, if you had a mortgage currently at 9 percent, you should wait until rates dropped to 7 percent before refinancing.

Today that rule of thumb makes little sense at all because of no-cost refinancing. Instead, it's a matter of every case judged on its own merits. Here's a way to determine what you should do.

1. *Determine what the refinance will cost.* If you get a zero-points and/or zero-cost mortgage, continue reading. If, however, it's going to cost you points and fees to get the mortgage, then you need to make some calculations. Skip down to number 3.

2. *Compare your old mortgage with your new one.* Some people feel that if the new zero-points/zero-cost mortgage is even $10 per month lower in payments, it worthwhile to go ahead. After all, it's not costing you anything *and* it's saving you money each month. But, that's a narrow way of looking at things and can land you in trouble. Other considerations are these:

   - *How old is your existing mortgage?* If you are in the latter years of the current mortgage, more of your payment will be going to principal. Converting to a new mortgage, more of your payment will be going to interest. It may make no sense to save a few dollars on the payment each month if you lose out on the equity return. On the other hand, you may be increasing the interest you can deduct from taxes.
   - *What types are the new and old mortgages?* Are you going from an adjustable rate to a fixed-rate mortgage? Or the other way round? If you're changing to an ARM, can the current low interest rate rise, thus defeating the purpose of the refinancing? If you're going to a fixed-rate, are you locking in a lower interest rate?
   - *Are you cashing out?* Taking money out of the property as part of the refinancing reduces your equity. That means you'll have less equity when it comes time to sell or when you need to refinance for an emergency.

3. *If you have closing costs/points, determine how long you will own the property.* Before refinancing, when you have costs and points, ask yourself how long until you break even. Will you be living in the property that long?

Questions to Ask to Determine Length of Ownership

1. Is a job change likely within a year or two? Yes[ ] No[ ]
2. Is your family outgrowing the home? Yes[ ] No[ ]
3. Are your kids grown up and leaving, making the home too big? Yes[ ] No[ ]
4. Are you likely to suffer a financial reversal (job loss, alimony reduction, or other income loss), making upkeep of the home difficult? Yes[ ] No[ ]
5. Is the property old and becoming obsolete so that you'd like to move to something newer? Yes[ ] No[ ]
6. Is the neighborhood declining, meaning you'll want to move soon? Yes[ ] No[ ]
7. Are there any other factors (health, marriage, and so on) that would force you to change your plans and move sooner? Yes[ ] No[ ]
8. Add up all your answers and take an educated, realistic guess: How long will you continue to live in the property?

The entire purpose of the quiz is to help you focus on the real possibility of wanting to sell the property and, more important, *when*. A lot of "yes" answers suggest that your stay in the property is likely to be short lived. If that's the case, try to come up with a date for selling that property.

Next, find out the total amount of your points and closing costs and divide them by the months before you anticipate selling. For example, if you anticipate selling within 36 months and your refinance fees are $3,600, that comes to $100 a month. This is the time to break even.

To determine the true costs of your mortgage, now add this amount to your new mortgage payment.

TIP

Keep in mind that this is a rough guess. Some of your points might be tax deductible over the life of the loan, which would affect the answer.

TIP

Don't cut it too fine. As noted, I have seen people refinance in order to save just $10 or $20 a month, which might not be worth the hassle.

What Are the Problems Associated with Refinancing?

Perhaps the biggest difficulty can be getting equity out. Lenders don't like to see you "cash out" your equity. In a typical refinance you'll have no trouble getting enough money to pay off the existing mortgage plus all of your costs of refinancing. But try to get a few dollars more and the lender may balk.

If you're an owner-occupant, you may find that many lenders will ease the above restriction, particularly if you have a lot of equity. However, if you're an investor, you'll find it very difficult to find lenders who will lend you equity-out money. You'll have to spend more time checking around.

Should I Get a Debt Consolidation Mortgage?

The motivation with a debt consolidation mortgage usually is to reduce the interest rate and payment while keeping the principal the same. It's typically done on credit card and personal loan (such as car) debt. A debt consolidation mortgage simply expresses the purpose of getting the financing.

The problem I have with this type of loan is that frequently what you're doing is converting short-term debt to long-term debt. For example, a car loan may be for four or five years. But, a new mortgage may be for 15 or 30 years. If you pay off the car with that long-term mortgage, you'll find you'll be making payments long after the car has gone to the scrap heap.

On the other hand, you may be in dire financial straits because of the many short-term, high interest rate loans you have and getting a single long-term mortgage (with a lower interest rate and payment) may be a way out. Just remember, however, that when you get a debt consolidation mortgage, you're usually eating up the equity in your house. It won't be there when you sell or when you want to refinance later.

TIP

If you have a lot of credit card debt, chances are that the new single mortgage payment will be significantly lower than the old numerous payments. When you add in car payments, however, this could change, because many times car loans are subsidized by manufacturers as an incentive to make the purchase. Your interest rate on a car loan just might be lower than the interest rate on the new consolidation loan. Be careful when you add in all the figures—you could be surprised.

What about Home Equity Loans?

A home equity loan is usually just another name for a second mortgage with a twist. The twist is that it's often a revolving loan. You have a maximum amount you can borrow. If you pay down the amount borrowed, you can borrow it again. Typically such revolving loans have a time limit, usually around 10 years, after which they switch to a nonrevolving loan. The remaining balance is usually in the form of an ARM paid back over 15 or 20 years.

Home equity loans are a great source of quick credit. Once set up, they're in place whenever you need them. Instead of having to borrow cash at very high interest rates (often 20 percent or more) on credit cards, you can borrow it on the home equity loan, typically for half that amount or less.

The drawback to this type of financing is that you must have considerable equity in your property. Your combined mortgages (including first and home equity second) usually cannot exceed 80 percent of the property value. Thus, if you already have a first mortgage currently at 70 percent of value, the maximum home equity loan you likely could get would be for 10 percent.

Generally speaking, you can use a home equity loan for any legal purpose. This includes college education, fixing up the property, or taking a cruise.

23

Understanding Adjustable Rate Mortgages

Adjustable rate mortgages, or ARMs, can provide many benefits to you, but unless you truly understand how they work, they can also result in trapping you into terms with which you might not be able to live. In this chapter we'll look at the ARM, both pro and con. And we'll try to figure out if it's really for you. (Remember, an ARM is a mortgage where the interest rate and, as a result, the monthly payment, are allowed to fluctuate.)

What's the Teaser Rate?

To induce borrowers to go with their ARM, lenders usually offer a "teaser." When a borrower asks how much the ARM's interest rate is, he or she is usually told the teaser rate, which may be as much as 2 or more points less than the current market rate. For example, the teaser rate may be 4 percent while the market rate for fixed mortgages is 6 percent. This is usually quite an inducement to borrowers to consider the ARM.

In point of fact, if an ARM offered the same interest rate as a fixed loan, few people would opt for it. The only way to get most people to go for the unpredictable interest rate and payments of the ARM is to induce them with the teaser.

Of course, lenders don't conceal the truth. If you apply for the ARM, you will be told what the true APR (annual percentage rate) is. This is a combination of the teaser rate and the market rate.

Teaser rates do not reflect what you ultimately will be paying in monthly payments. The teaser can last for as short a time as a month, or as long as several years.

TRAP

Some borrowers think (regardless of what lenders may say) that if interest rates go down on an ARM, their payments automatically will likewise go down. This may not be the case for your ARM. If you get a low teaser rate, you are already paying substantially below market interest. The market rate would have to go down to below your teaser rate just for your payments to remain constant. If the market rate goes down, but not as far as your teaser, your payments may still have to rise. If the market rate stays the same, your payments may have to rise even more playing catch-up.

TIP

If you are going to hold the property a short time and then sell or refinance, an ARM with a good teaser may be the better loan for you. You will benefit from the low teaser rate, and then (it is hoped) will sell or refinance the property before the ARM's interest rate (and payment) rises. Just be sure that your teaser rate lasts long enough.

Keep in mind that the teaser is temporary. It will change in time, often in a very short time.

Beware of Underqualifying Because of Teasers

A worst-case scenario comes about when we are underqualified for a mortgage because of the teaser rate. Lenders in the distant past qualified borrowers, not on the market interest rate of the mortgage, but rather on the basis of the lower teaser rate. It's much easier to qualify at the lower interest rate and payments. The unfortunate result was that borrowers couldn't handle the payments when the teaser ended and the interest rate and payments moved up.

In the ARM market today, however, most lenders are refusing to qualify borrowers at the teaser rate. However, they are not necessarily qualifying them at the current market rate either. Many use a complex formula that qualifies them somewhere in between.

Be sure you understand how your lender is qualifying you. And be sure you can truly afford the mortgage before you get it.

TIP

Be sure to ask your lender, "What will my monthly payment be once the teaser rate is gone?" Can you live with it?

What's the Index?

Each ARM is tied to an index that reflects the cost of borrowing money. The interest rate on your mortgage goes up or down as does the index it's tied to. You often have a choice on which index to use (if by no other way than switching lenders). That's an important decision.

The most commonly used indexes are as follows:

A.   One-Year Treasury Security Index
B.   11th District Cost of Funds Index (COFI)
C.   Two- Three-, Five-, or Seven-Year Treasury Security Index
D.   Prime Rate Index
E.   LIBOR (London Interbank Offered Rate) Index

TIP

Lenders want their ARMs tied to indexes that record volatility in the market. You, on the other hand, usually want your ARM tied to an index that moves slowly, if at all, so your rate and monthly payment stay fairly constant.

Finding the right index is often one of the most important decisions when you select an ARM. The following is an explanation of what each of these different indexes covers.

One-Year Treasury Security Index

The most popular index with lenders is the One-Year Treasury Security Index. It is based on the weekly average yield on U.S. Treasury securities. When you hear about interest rates rising or falling, this is what is often being referred to. Changes in monetary and economic conditions usually will be reflected in this rate and will then be quickly transmitted to your ARM. This index is a fairly volatile one.

COFI:11th District Cost of Funds Index

This is the 11th Federal Home Loan Bank District, which comprises California, Arizona, and Nevada. It measures the cost to financial institutions located in the 11th District when they try to attract deposits. It reflects the weighted average cost of borrowings, advances, and savings of these financial institutions. This is less volatile than other indexes (it's slow to rise and slow to fall). Borrowers like it during periods when interest rates are rising. It is used nationally.

Two-, Three-. Five-, or Seven-Year Treasury Security Index

Depending on your loan, and on how often the rate is adjusted, your index might be the "yield on United States Treasury Securities adjusted to a constant maturity of _____ years," where the blank could be two, three, five, or even seven years or longer.

This refers to the constant maturity of Treasury securities for whatever year is selected. The longer period of time tends to make these somewhat more stable than the One-Year Treasury Security Index. These indexes are calculated either weekly or monthly, and they can have different values, depending on which is used.

Prime Rate Index

The prime rate is the best rate that banks charge their best customers for short-term borrowing. The rate often will vary by as much as half a point between lenders. Therefore, when used as an index, the composite prime rate as reported in the *Wall Street Journal* is usually given. This rate tends to be fairly stable, but when it does move, it tends to move in large chunks.

LIBOR Index

Almost no one outside of the lending industry has heard of the London Interbank Offered Rate, or LIBOR. It is the rate that banks in the London area use when they borrow sizeable amounts from other nearby banks. It is one of the oldest indexes and most commonly used for short-term loans. It tends to be more volatile than COFI but less so than the one-year Treasury security. It is popular because it has an international appeal and isn't entirely linked to U.S. securities.

TIP

When a lender offers you an index, it is required to show you the history of the index going back several years. Just be sure that the index history covers the most volatile interest rate period of 1978 to 1982. Those years will tell you more than any others about what this index is likely to do if and when interest rates skyrocket.

There are other indexes used. No matter which your lender opts for, it is important to get a history of how that index has performed over time. This can help you see just how volatile it is.

Your lender should provide you with the index history. However, you can quickly find histories for a variety of indexes using the Internet. Try a good search engine using the keywords *mortgage index*. One source that I have found useful is www.hsh.com/idxhst.html.

How Do I Decide Which Index to Use?

Some lenders give you a choice. If they don't, you can shop lenders until you find one who uses an index you want. Generally speaking, most borrowers want to pick a lender and an index that shows stability over time.

Be careful. An index that is volatile but is down when you apply may give you a better beginning interest rate than an index that is stable but stays up.

TIP

If you plan to keep the mortgage a long time, you should probably go for the index that is most stable. If you plan to keep the mortgage a short time, consider an index that is currently the lowest.

What's the Margin?

The interest rate you pay on your mortgage is not simply the index interest rate. Rather, the lender will add a "margin" to the index to determine your actual mortgage interest rate. For example, the lender may specify in your ARM documents that the margin is 2.5 percent. That means that when the index is 4 percent, for example, the lender adds the margin of 2.5 percent to the 4 percent and you have an effective mortgage interest rate of 6.5 percent.

The margin is tied directly to the index used. If the index is generally low, the lender will tend to use a higher margin. If the index is generally high, the lender will tend to use a lower margin.

TRAP

Don't trust lenders to look out for you. Ask to see the performance of the margin on its index going back at least 10 years. See how well this index performed with the margin the lender uses. Compare it to fixed interest rates for the same period (something the lender should also supply). Would you end up paying market interest rates most of the time? Or would you pay higher-than-market rates? It's worth spending some time investigating.

What Is the Adjustment Period?

The adjustment period is how frequently the lender can adjust the mortgage rate up or down.

Typical ARM Adjustment Periods

- Monthly
- Bimonthly
- Three months
- Six months
- Annually (most popular recently)
- Biannually
- Every three years
- Every five years

TIP

Most of the time you will want the longest adjustment periods possible. This gives you the greatest stability. However, most of the time lenders want the shortest adjustment periods. This gives them the greatest protection against interest rate hikes. Therefore, when shopping for a mortgage, it is highly advisable to place the adjustment period as a big priority on the list of terms for which to look.

What about Interest/Payment Rate Caps?

Lenders are aware of borrowers' fears of hikes in ARM payments caused by big jumps in the market interest rate. If the mortgage were allowed to rise without restriction, in a very volatile market we might start out paying 5 percent and end up paying 10 percent or more. As a result our monthly payments could double as well. Few borrowers would go for a mortgage with such a downside risk.

To help reduce borrowers' fears, lenders frequently put "caps" on the ARM interest rate. A cap is a limit on the amount the interest rate, the monthly payment, or both can rise (or fall). For example, if there were a 4 percent cap on the interest rate, it couldn't rise (or fall) by more than 4 percent. If the market rate rose higher, the ARM would be limited and wouldn't respond.

TIP

The cap puts both a ceiling and a floor on the ARM. The interest rate can't go above a certain amount. But it can't go below a certain amount either. If the cap is 5 percent, for example, the rate can rise above or fall below 5 percent of the current rate. Keep in mind that that amounts to a swing of 10 percent.

Are Interest Rate Caps Beneficial?

Most borrowers would agree that interest rate caps are beneficial. Yes, they would say, we want to be protected against runaway interest rates and runaway monthly payments. However, interest rate caps are deceptive. They usually don't really give as much protection as they seem to. The reason is that they are often set so high. For them to kick in, often interest rates would have to reach dramatic highs. Caps are more for protection over the long term than for month-to-month payments.

What about Monthly Payment Caps?

Some ARMs set a maximum limit on the amount the monthly payment can be raised each adjustment period regardless of what happens to the interest rate. Many borrowers like this arrangement, since it limits their monthly payment increases regardless of what interest rates do. However, it can also be a trap. The reason is that if the interest rate rises faster than the monthly payment, there's interest that doesn't get paid each month. This is then usually added to the principal of the mortgage. In other words, the mortgage amount (the principal) grows!

Effect of Capping the Mortgage Payment
$100,000 mortgage for 30 years with 7.5 percent payment cap. Assume the interest rate rises 2 percent.

Increase in mortgage payment required to handle the interest rate increase	$151
Maximum payment increase allowed	−$66
Shortfall added to mortgage	$85

Without the payment cap, the mortgage payment would rise $151. With it, the maximum rise is $66, and $85 is now added to the principal owed on the mortgage.

"Negative amortization" is when the mortgage increases rather than decreases. As a result, you end up paying interest on interest. Most government mortgages allow up to 25 percent of the mortgage amount to be added interest. In other words, you can end up owing up to 125 percent of what you borrowed because of negative amortization.

Negative amortization often is not thoroughly explained to borrowers. Unless you know what to look for in the documents, you might not spot it. Although the negative amortization terms are usually explained in those mortgages in which it occurs, many people simply don't understand the implications. Many people still fail to see the dangers.

TRAP

Negative amortization means that instead of the mortgage going down, it goes up. Each month instead of paying off some of the loan, you add to it. You end up owing more than you originally borrowed with the result that you are paying interest on interest.

How Do You Find Out If Your Mortgage Has Negative Amortization?

Look for a payment cap. If your mortgage has one, you can be fairly sure that negative amortization is a possibility.

Finally, the ultimate monthly payment with a cap may be higher than without. Consider the following example prepared by the Federal Home Loan Bank Board. In this case, various interest rate caps are given and the monthly payment is shown over a period of 29 years. The chart was prepared during a period of very high interest rates. Nonetheless, its assumptions remain valid for lower interest rate periods as well. It assumes that interest rates start at 12 percent, then rise to 18 percent at year 5, and remain there.

Notice that the lower the monthly payment cap, the lower the monthly payments initially. But over the long run, the lower the monthly payment cap, the higher the monthly payments as the lender plays catch-up trying to recoup interest not received because of the payment cap.

Cap Rate Comparison Chart
($50,000 30-year mortgage)

Year	Interest rate	Monthly payment			
		7% cap	7.5% cap	10% cap	No cap
1	12	514	514	514	514
2	13.5	540	552	565	572
3	15	567	594	622	630
4	16.5	595	638	684	689
5	18	625	686	753	748
6	"	656	738	"	"
10	"	797	800	"	"
15	"	1018	"	"	"
20	"	1112	"	"	"
25	"	"	"	"	"
29	"	"	"	"	"

TIP

Monthly payment caps can mean lower monthly payments now but higher monthly payments later on.

The preceding example overlooked an important consideration: A mortgage might have *both* a monthly payment cap *and* an interest rate cap.

When a mortgage has both an interest rate cap and a monthly payment cap, you automatically should check to see whether the interest rate cap is set higher than the monthly payment cap. If it is, negative amortization could take place. The reason is simple: If this weren't the case, if the interest rate cap were set sufficiently low that no negative amortization could take place, then no monthly payment cap would be necessary.

What Are the Steps?

Many ARMs also set a maximum limit on the amount the interest can be raised each adjustment period. For example, many ARMs have a 1 or 2 percent maximum interest rate adjustment. That means that regardless of what the real interest rate has moved, the interest rate on the mortgage can only be adjusted in steps of 1 or 2 percent.

To see how steps work, let's say interest rates on our index have gone through the roof. Can an ARM interest rate in one adjustment period be raised to its maximum cap? If the original rate (as per our example) was 5 percent and the cap was 5 percent, can the interest rate be hiked upward to 10 percent in one adjustment period?

If the loan did not have steps, then the answer would be yes. However, nearly all ARMs have steps that limit the hikes in interest rate per each adjustment period. These limits are typically anywhere from ½ percent to 2½ percent per adjustment period. Thus, regardless of what the index the mortgage is tied to may do, the interest rate cannot be hiked more than the step amount each period.

The smaller the steps, the greater the lag time when there is a sudden jump in interest rates. (Of course, a sudden decline would not be felt as quickly, either.) If we assume that interest rates will tend to move both up and down, the smaller the steps, therefore, the more stable the mortgage monthly payment tends to be. From a practical perspective, the steps can often have a far greater impact on the stability of the mortgage than can an interest rate cap.

Ideally, you usually would want a mortgage with small steps over one with larger payment caps.

TRAP

Many ARM lenders are naturally concerned about the lag in mortgages with small steps. They see that they could lose out on interest during spikes in interest rates. As a consequence, some ARMs are written with "catch-up clauses." These clauses provide that even though the step doesn't rise fast enough to keep pace with the index, any interest lost to the lender in this fashion would be carried over to the next adjustment period. With a catch-up clause in a mortgage, the beneficial effects to the borrower of smaller steps are nullified over a long period of time.

TIP

Shop for a lender who offers both small steps and no catch-up clauses. They are hard to find, but they do exist in many markets. On the other hand, avoid mortgages with catch-up clauses if at all possible.

Lenders like ARMs because they reduce the lender's concerns over interest rate volatility. Agents like them because they help make sales that otherwise might fall through. Borrowers like them because they mean initially lower payments and the ability to get financing that otherwise might not be available.

But don't think of them as a panacea. They are not. They can solve a particular mortgage problem that you might have. But they won't solve all of your problems. And, after a few years, they could end up causing more difficulty than the problem they originally seemed to cure.

24

How Do I Prepare for the Loan Closing?

Once you are successful in obtaining a mortgage, a time will come when the lender will want you to sign papers. Typically you'll go down to an escrow office (or to the office of the real estate attorney who's handling the escrow) and there you'll be given a stack of papers to sign. If it's a refinance, they will just be loan documents. On the other hand, if the mortgage is part of a purchase, there may be other documents involved in the purchase to sign as well.

Should you bring anything or anyone with you to the closing? Should you just sign everything on faith? What should you dispute, if anything? These are the questions that most people ask at a closing, and we're going to take brief look at some of them and their answers.

Who Should I Take to the Closing?

Unless you're well versed in real estate and finance, it's a good idea to bring someone who is. This could be a real estate agent, an attorney, a financial counselor—a person who knows the ropes and who will put your interests first.

229

TRAP

Often at closings the borrower has many questions about the loan documents. However, the escrow officer handling the closing may not know the correct answers or may be unwilling to advise on legal matters. This could be the case for real estate agents as well. If that's the case, your best bet may be a knowledgeable friend or attorney.

TIP

If you aren't sure about something, it's usually a good idea to wait until you get an answer that satisfies you. If the loan is part of a purchase, just keep in mind, however, that waiting could jeopardize the transaction and land you in hot water with the seller. And with purchase or refinance, waiting can also sometimes jeopardize getting the financing. If there's an error, keep in mind that while it may be possible to change it after you sign, it's so much easier to take care of it before you sign.

What Should I Bring to the Closing?

The lender will let you know. You may need your checkbook if you want to write a personal check to cover items such as fees and points. Even though these may be covered by the mortgage, having a check to show that you personally paid for them might be of some help if certain tax problems occur. (See Chapter 21.)

In addition, if you're getting a mortgage online, the lender may want to see promised documentation such as W-2 forms, bank statements, paycheck stubs, and so forth. Whatever you're asked to bring, be sure you bring it with you. Otherwise, the whole process may be delayed for days (during which the lender may eventually charge you for the delay) until you have everything.

TRAP

Anything but an electronic transfer of money will result in a delay. Even a cashier's check may take several days to clear.

What Should I Challenge?

Carefully read the fees and charges. You should have been made aware of these early on in a good faith estimate when you applied for the mortgage. If you're not sure what statement you should have gotten or what to challenge, reread Chapter 9. These are things best handled long before the closing, but if you find something out of line even now, it may be worthwhile to bring it to the closing officer's attention.

TIP

Double-check the math. In the old days (read: before computers), closing agents were constantly making errors. Today that's much rarer. However, it does still happen. Be sure all the columns add up. Perhaps just as important, be sure that the credits and debits are properly given. If the seller agreed to pay one of your loan points and instead you're shown as paying them all, point out the error and have it corrected on the spot. It won't take but a few minutes for a computer to spit out new and correct documents.

If you're self-employed, you may want to pay special attention to IRS Form 4506, which the lender may ask you to sign. This form allows the lender to check with the IRS to confirm that the copies of tax returns you submitted with your application are the same as those you filed with the IRS.

The lender's concern is understandable. However, I have heard of cases where the lenders have not properly filled out Form 4506. Namely, they have left out the date as well as the name of the party to whom the information is to be released. If you sign the form with these two areas blank, you are virtually signing away your privacy. Anyone's name could go into the blank, and the form could be dated well into the future.

I suspect the reason the lender wants these two areas blank is that the lender is going to sell the mortgage on the secondary market or assign it to another lender. At the time you sign, the lender may not know the future holder of the loan, so the name is left blank. Additionally, since the lender doesn't know how long it will be before the transfer is completed, and since the form is only good for 60 days after the date, the lender wants that blank as well.

What can you do? This is one of those situations that you will find hard to anticipate. This form undoubtedly won't be shown to you until you're ready to sign. By then, it's going to be tough to stop everything and get another lender. Besides, who's to say another lender won't want the same form signed?

I am self-employed and, when faced with this situation, I have filled in the name and dated the form. Thus far, lenders have not refused to give me financing because of doing so. Of course, your situation could be different.

TIP

If you're self-employed, talk to your mortgage broker or loan representative. Bring up Form 4506, and express your concern at the time you apply for the mortgage. Explain that you are willing to sign, which should allay the lender's concern about your having fudged some documents. But also explain the privacy issue and say you won't sign a form that's not fully filled out. By preparing for the situation in advance, you may be able to get the lender to agree to fill out the form. Or if the lender won't, you should then have time to find another lender.

TRAP

Would you sign a blank check? If the answer is no (as it should be), then why should you be forced to sign a blank IRS document? Either way, it could lead to all kinds of unforeseen problems.

What Will I Need to Sign?

You'll be expected to sign the loan agreement. That can mean signing several documents, including the following:

- Deed of trust
- Mortgage
- Loan agreement
- Ancillary documents

You should expect everything to be explained to you. You may find that some of the documents are dozens of pages long and filled with tiny print.

TIP

I encourage you to read everything, no matter how small the typeface or apparently insignificant the material. You may find some onerous terms to which you would never agree. Or you may find that the lender has slipped in a clause that you and the lender had previously agreed would not be there. You may have to have the clause deleted and initialed (although it's much more likely that the lender will want to have the documents redrawn from scratch).

Don't be concerned if it takes an hour or more to read what you are expected to sign. You're center stage, and nothing happens until you sign. Once you sign, however, your role diminishes greatly. Although others may complain, everyone usually will wait while you read it, or they will make arrangements so you have the time and an area to read it.

Remember, you hold the leverage—until you sign. Then, you're the borrower with the lender's mortgage around your neck.

Amortization Table

Use the following table to determine the approximate monthly mortgage payment (principal and interest) when you already know the loan amount. Just multiply the loan amount by the factor at the given interest rate and you'll be given the monthly payment.

Interest	Years				
	3	5	10	15	30
5.00	.029972	.018871	.010607	.007907	.005368
5.25	.030082	.018986	.010729	.008039	.005522
5.50	.030196	.019101	.010853	.008171	.005678
5.75	.030309	.019218	.010977	.008304	.005356
6.00	.030422	.019333	.011102	.008439	.005996
6.25	.030535	.019449	.011228	.008574	.006157
6.50	.030649	.019566	.011354	.008711	.006321
6.75	.030763	.019684	.011482	.008849	.006480
7.00	.030877	.019801	.011610	.008988	.006653
7.25	.030991	.019919	.011740	.009129	.006822
7.50	.031106	.020037	.011870	.009270	.006992
7.75	.031221	.020157	.012001	.009413	.007164
8.00	.031336	.020276	.012133	.009557	.007338
8.25	.031341	.020396	.012265	.009701	.007513
8.50	.031567	.020516	.012399	.009847	.007689
8.75	.041683	.020637	.012533	.009995	.007867
9.00	.031799	.020758	.012668	.010143	.008046
9.25	.031916	.020879	.012802	.010292	.008227
9.50	.032032	.021001	.012940	.010442	.008409
9.75	.032149	.021124	.013077	.010594	.008592
10.00	.032267	.021247	.013215	.010746	.008776
10.25	.032385	.021370	.013354	.010896	.008961
10.50	.032502	.021494	.013494	.011054	.009147
10.75	.032621	.021618	.013634	.011210	.009335
11.00	.032739	.021742	.013775	.011366	.009523
11.25	.032857	.021867	.013917	.011523	.009713
11.50	.032976	.021993	.014060	.011682	.009903
11.75	.033095	.022118	.014203	.011841	.010094
12.00	.033214	.022244	.014347	.012002	.010286
12.25	.033334	.022371	.014492	.012163	.010479
12.50	.033454	.022498	.014638	.012325	.010673
12.75	.033574	.022625	.014784	.012488	.010867
13.00	.033694	.022753	.014931	.012652	.011062
13.25	.033815	.022881	.015079	.012817	.011258
13.50	.033935	.023010	.015227	.012983	.011454
13.75	.034056	.023139	.015377	.013150	.011651
14.00	.034178	.023268	.015527	.013317	.011849

Note: You can also quickly and easily get the payment amount by going online and using the calculator at any of the Internet mortgage services such as eloan.com, lendingtree.com, mortgage.com, and so on.

Mortgage Terms

If borrowing a mortgage is something that's new to you, the first thing you're going to discover is that lenders speak a different language. There are "points" and "origination fees" and "alienation clauses" and dozens of other terms that can make you think they're talking Chinese.

While this should simply be a tiny stumbling block that can be quickly overcome with occasionally humorous results (over terms you don't understand), too often the real consequences are that borrowers don't get the best loan because they don't understand the terminology. If you don't speak "mortgage-ese" and you let this hinder you, you could end up paying a great deal more for your home financing than you need to.

To help you overcome the mystery of the hidden language of mortgage, here are some of the most important terms and their definitions. Knowing these essential terms will help you make intelligent decisions in real estate.

Mortgage Versus Trust Deeds

Before actually looking at mortgage terms, let's clear up one important point. In this book the term *mortgage* is used to mean any financing that you get that is secured by real estate.

In the distant past, almost all of this type of financing was called a mortgage, hence the widespread understanding and use of the term today. However, during the latter half of this century, particularly in

California, a different type of mortgage instrument came into existence called the "trust deed." Today, chances are if you secure financing on your property, you will get a trust deed, not a mortgage. Consequently, it's important to take a few moments to understand the differences between the two types of loan instruments.

Mortgage

There are two parties to a mortgage: the borrower, or *mortgagor*, and the lender or *mortgagee*. Skipping to an eventuality that most of us don't like to consider, the big difference between a mortgage and trust deed has to do with foreclosure.

If we don't make our payments on a mortgage, the lender can only foreclose, or take ownership of the property, by going to court. This court action can take a great deal of time, often six months or more. Further, even after the lender has taken back the property, we as borrowers may have an "equity of redemption" that allows us to redeem the property sometimes for years after we've lost it by paying back the mortgage and the lender's costs. The length of time it takes to foreclose, the costs involved, and the equity of redemption make mortgages undesirable to lenders.

Trust Deed

Trust deeds came into use in the early part of this century, primarily in California, by clever and enterprising lenders. If you wanted to borrow money from them, they would say, "Yes, I'll loan you money on your property. But to insure that my money is guaranteed, you sign a deed over to me. I won't record the deed unless you don't pay."

We borrowers, of course, wouldn't stand for that. If we gave the lender the deed to our property, he or she could take ownership at any time. So the lenders compromised. They said, "Okay, make the deed out to an independent third party, a stake holder. That third party will hold the deed and will sign it over to us only if you don't make your payments." That seemed fair, and borrowers went along with it. Over time, the trust deed, as it came to be called, was codified into law.

There are three parties to a trust deed: the borrower, or "trustor"; the independent third party, the stake holder, called the "trustee" (usually a title insurance company); and the lender, called the "beneficiary," since the lender stands to benefit if the trustee turns the deed over in the event we fail to make our payments.

The advantage of the trust deed over the mortgage is that foreclosure can be accomplished without court action. The beneficiary (lender) simply informs the trustee that we haven't made our payments, and the trustee issues the lender a deed.

Of course, strict procedures must be followed. In California, for example, the lender must allow the borrower 90 days to make the loan current. Then it must advertise the property for 21 days, during which time we can redeem the loan by paying it back. Finally, it must "sell" the property to the highest bidder (usually the lender) on the courthouse steps.

Nevertheless, the process is relatively fast, there are no court costs, and we have no equity of redemption once the trustee sale is made. Once title passes from the trustee to the beneficiary (lender), we lose all interest in the property.

One other point needs to be mentioned. With trust deed foreclosure, there can be no deficiency judgment. In other words, if the property is worth less than the loan, the lender can't come back to us for the difference. In judicial foreclosure, in some instances, the lender can. For this reason, some lenders who hold a trust deed will opt for judicial foreclosure rather than trustee foreclosure. (See also Purchase Money Mortgage later in this appendix.)

Note: In this book the terms *trust deeds* and *mortgages* are used synonymously.

Terms Used in Mortgages

Now let's move forward to consider the most important terms used in *securing* mortgages on single-family residential property.

Abstract of Title

This is a written document produced by a title insurance company (in some states an attorney will do it) giving the history of who owned the property from the first owner forward. It also indicates any liens or encumbrances that may affect the title. A lender will not make a loan nor can a sale normally conclude until the title to real estate is clear, as evidenced by the abstract.

Acceleration Clause

This "accelerates" the payments in a mortgage, meaning that the entire amount becomes immediately due and payable. Most mortgages have this clause, which kicks in if, for example, you sell the property. (Also called an "alienation clause.")

Adjustable Rate Mortgage (ARM)

The interest rate on this mortgage fluctuates up or down according to an index and a margin agreed to in advance by the borrower and the lender. In some cases when there are limits to the amount of change that can be made to the payment, a charge may actually be made to the principal. (See Negative Amortization.)

Adjustment Date

This is the day on which an adjustment is made in an adjustable rate mortgage. It may occur monthly, every six months, once a year, or as otherwise agreed.

Alienation Clause

This is a clause in a mortgage that usually specifies if you sell or transfer the property to another person, the mortgage becomes immediately due and payable. (Also called an "acceleration clause.")

ALTA

American Land Title Association. This is a more complete and extensive policy of title insurance that most lenders insist upon. It involves a physical inspection and often guarantees the property's boundaries. Lenders will often insist on an ALTA policy with themselves named a beneficiary.

Amortization

This refers to paying back the mortgage in equal installments. In other words, if the mortgage is for 30 years, you would have 360 equal installments. (The last payment is often a few dollars more or less.) This is opposed to a balloon payment in which one payment is larger than the rest.

Annual Percentage Rate (APR)

This tells you the actual rate you will pay including interest, loan fees, and points according to the government.

Appraisal

Lenders usually require that the property be appraised by a qualified appraiser. The amount of the appraisal is the maximum value on which the loan will be based. For example, if the appraisal is $100,000 and the lender will loan 80 percent of value, the maximum mortgage would be $80,000.

ASA

American Society of Appraisers. An appraiser who displays this designation belongs to this professional organization.

Assignment of Mortgage

The lender may sell your mortgage without your permission. For example, you may obtain a mortgage from XYZ savings and loan. It may then sell that mortgage to Bland Bank. You will then get a letter saying the mortgage was assigned, and you make your payments to a new entity. The document used between lenders for the transfer is an "assignment of mortgage." (*Note:* Beware of receiving any letter saying you should send your mortgage payment elsewhere. Unscrupulous individuals have sent out such letters to borrowers in the hopes of cheating them out of payments. Verify any such letters with your old lender.)

Assumption

This means to take over an existing mortgage. For example, a seller may have an "assumable" mortgage on a property. When you buy the property, you take over that seller's obligation under the loan. Today most fixed-rate mortgages are not assumable. Most adjustable rate mortgages are, but the borrower must qualify. FHA and VA mortgages may be assumable, but certain conditions may have to be met. When you assume the mortgage, you are liable if there is a foreclosure.

Automatic Guarantee

Some lenders who make VA loans are empowered to guarantee the loans without first checking with the VA. These lenders can often make the loans quicker.

Balloon Payment

One payment, usually the last, on a mortgage is larger than the others. In the case of second mortgages held by sellers, often only interest is paid until the due date—then the entire amount borrowed (the principal) is due.

Biweekly Mortgage

You make your payments every other week instead of monthly. Since there are 52 weeks in the year, you end up making 26 payments, or the equivalent of one month's extra payment. The additional payment significantly reduces the amount of interest charged on the mortgage and often reduces the term of the loan.

Blanket Mortgage

Here you have one mortgage that covers several properties instead of a single mortgage for each property. It is used most frequently by developers and builders.

Buy-Down Mortgage

You receive a lower-than-market interest rate either for the entire term of the mortgage or for a set period at the beginning, say two years. This is made possible by the builder or seller paying an upfront fee to the lender.

Call Provision

A clause in the mortgage allowing the lender to call in the entire unpaid balance of the loan providing certain events have occurred, such as your selling the property. (Also called an "acceleration clause" and an "alienation clause.")

Caps

These are limits put on an adjustable rate mortgage. The interest rate, the monthly payment, or both may be capped.

Certificate of Reasonable Value (CRV)

When getting a VA loan, the Veterans Administration will secure an appraisal of the property and will issue this document establishing what they feel is its maximum value. In some cases, you may not pay more than this amount and still get the VA loan.

Chain of Title

This gives the history of ownership of the property. The title to property forms a chain going back to the first owners, which in the Southwest, for example, may come from original Spanish land grants.

Closing

This occurs when the seller conveys title to the buyer and the buyer makes full payment, including financing, for the property. Closing means the deal is consummated or concluded, all required documents are signed and delivered, and funds are disbursed.

Commitment

When a lender issues a written promise to you as a borrower to offer a mortgage at a set amount, interest rate, and cost. Typically commitments have a time limit on them—for example, they are good for 30 days or 60 days. Some lenders charge for making a commitment if you don't subsequently take out the mortgage (since they have tied up the money for that amount of time). When the lender's offer is in writing, it is sometimes called a "firm commitment."

Construction Loan

A mortgage made for the purpose of constructing a building. The loan is short term, typically under 12 months, and is usually paid in installments directly to the builder as the work is completed. Usually it is interest-only.

Conventional Loan

Any loan that is not government guaranteed or insured.

Convertible Mortgage

This is an adjustable rate mortgage (ARM) that contains a clause allowing it to be converted to a fixed-rate mortgage at some time in the future. You may have to pay an additional cost to obtain this mortgage.

Cosigner

If you don't have good enough credit to qualify for a mortgage, the lender may be willing to make the loan if you have someone with better credit (usually a close relative) also sign. This cosigner is equally responsible with you for repayment of the loan. (Even if you don't pay it back, the cosigner can be responsible for the *entire* balance.)

Credit Report

This is a report of your credit history usually made by one of the country's three large credit reporting companies. It will typically state if you have any delinquent payments or any failures to pay, as well as any bankruptcies and, sometimes, foreclosures. Lenders use it to determine whether to offer you a mortgage. The fee is usually under $50 and charged to you.

Discount

This has two meanings. When you borrow from a lender, the lender may withhold enough money from the mortgage to cover the points and fees. For example, you may be borrowing $100,000, but your points and fees come to $3,000; hence, the lender will only fund $97,000, discounting the $3,000.

In the secondary market a discount is the amount less than face value a buyer of a mortgage pays in order to be induced to purchase it. The discount here is calculated on the basis of risk, market rates, interest rate of the note, and other factors.

Due-on-Encumbrance Clause

This is a little-noted and seldom-enforced clause in many recent mortgages that allows the lender to foreclose if you, the borrower, get additional financing. For example, if you secure a second mortgage, the lender of the first mortgage with the clause may have grounds for foreclosing. The reasoning here is that the lender wants you to have a certain level of equity in the property. If you reduce your equity level by taking out additional financing, the lender may be placed in a less secure position.

Due-on-Sale Clause

This is a clause in a mortgage that says the entire remaining unpaid balance becomes due and payable on sale of the property. (See also Acceleration Clause.)

Escrow Company

The escrow is the stake holder—an independent third party that handles funds; carries out the instructions of the lender, buyer, and seller in a transaction; and deals with all the documents. In most states, companies are licensed to handle escrows. In some parts of the country, particularly the Northeast, the function of the escrow company may be handled by an attorney.

FHA Loan

A mortgage insured by the Federal Housing Administration. In most cases FHA advances no money but instead insures the loan to a lender such as a bank. There is a fee to the borrower, usually paid up front, for this insurance.

Graduated Payment Mortgage

Here the payments you make vary over the life of the loan. They start out low, then slowly rise until, usually after a few years, they reach a plateau where they remain for the remainder of the term. This mortgage is particularly useful when you want low initial payments. It is primarily used by first-time buyers. It often is used in combination with a fixed-rate or an adjustable rate mortgage.

Growing Equity Mortgage

This is a rarely used type of mortgage where the payments increase according to a set schedule. The purpose is to pay additional money into principal and thus pay off the loan earlier and save interest charges.

Index

An index is a measurement of an established interest rate used to establish the periodic rate adjustments for adjustable rate mortgages. There are a wide variety of indexes used including Treasury Bill rates, cost of funds to lenders, and others.

Lien

A claim for money against real estate. For example, if you had work done on your property and refused to pay the workperson, he or she might file a "mechanic's lien" against your property. If you didn't pay taxes, the taxing agency might file a "tax lien." These liens "cloud" the title and usually prevent you from selling the property or refinancing it until they are cleared by paying off the debt.

Loan-to-Value Ratio

The percentage of the appraised value of a property that a lender will loan. For example, if your property appraised at $100,000 and the lender was willing to loan $80,000, then the loan-to-value ratio would be 80 percent.

MAI

American Institute of Real Estate Appraisers. An appraiser who has this designation has passed rigorous training.

Margin

An amount, calculated in points, that a lender adds to an index to determine how much interest you will pay during a period for an adjustable rate mortgage. For example, the index may be at 7 percent, and the margin, agreed upon at the time you obtained the mortgage, may be 2.7 points. The interest rate for that period, therefore, would be 9.7 percent.

Negative Amortization

Negative amortization occurs when the payment on an adjustable rate mortgage is not sufficiently large to cover the interest charged. When this happens, the excess interest is added to the principal, thus the amount borrowed actually increases. The amount the principal can increase is usually limited to 125 percent of the original mortgage value. *Anytime you have a cap on the mortgage payment,* you are looking at a mortgage that has the potential to be negatively amortized.

Origination Fee

Today this usually refers to the costs to you when you obtain a mortgage. In the past it has meant a charge that lenders make for preparing and submitting a mortgage. It originally was used only for FHA and VA loans where the mortgage package had to be submitted to the government for approval. With an FHA loan the maximum origination fee used to be 1 percent.

Personal Property

Any property that does not go with the land. This includes automobiles, clothing, and most furniture. Some items are disputable, such as appliances and floor and wall coverings. (See the related discussion under Real Property.)

PITI

This is an acronym for principal, interest, taxes, and insurance, the major components that go into determining your monthly payment on a mortgage. (They leave out other items such as homeowner's dues, utilities, and so forth.)

Points

A point is equal to 1 percent of a mortgage amount. For example, if your mortgage was $100,000 and you were required to pay 2½ points to get it, the charge to you would be $2,500. Some points that you pay when obtaining a mortgage may be tax deductible.

Lenders use the term *basis points*. A "basis point" is ⅟₁₀₀ of a point. For example, if you are charged ½ point (½ percent of the mortgage), the lender will think of it as 50 basis points.

Prepayment Penalty

This is a charge made by the lender to the borrower for paying off a mortgage early. In times past (more than 25 years ago) nearly all mortgages carried prepayment penalties. However, those mortgages were also assumable by others. Today virtually no fixed-rate mortgages (other than FHA or VA) are truly assumable and, hence, almost none carry a prepayment penalty clause.

Private Mortgage Insurance (PMI)

PMI is insurance that protects the lender in the event you default on a mortgage. It is written by an independent third-party insurance company and typically covers only the first 18 or 37 percent of the lender's potential loss. PMI is normally required on any mortgage that exceeds 80 percent loan-to-value ratio.

Purchase Money Mortgage

When you get a mortgage as part of the purchase price of a home (usually from the seller) rather than through refinancing, it's called a "purchase money mortgage." In some states, no deficiency judgment can be obtained against a borrower of a purchase money mortgage. (If there is a foreclosure and the property brings less than the amount borrowed, you, as a borrower, cannot be held liable for the shortfall.)

Real Property

Another word for real estate. This includes the land and anything appurtenant to it, including the house. Confusion often exists when differentiating between real and personal property with regard to such items as floor and wall covering. To determine whether an item is real property (goes with the land), certain tests have been devised. For example, if curtains or drapes have been attached in such a way that they cannot be removed without damaging the home, they may be spoken of a real property. On the other hand, if they can easily be removed without damaging the home, they may be personal property. It is a good idea to specify in any contract whether items are real or personal. This avoids confusion later on.

RESPA

An acronym for Real Estate Settlement Procedures Act. This act requires lenders to provide you with specified information as to the cost of securing financing. Basically it means that before you proceed far along the path of getting the mortgage, the lender has to provide you with an estimate of costs. Then, before you actually sign the documents binding you to the mortgage, the lender has to provide you with a breakdown of the actual costs.

Second Mortgage

An inferior mortgage usually placed on the property after a first mortgage. In the event of foreclosure, this mortgage would be paid off with funds from a foreclosure sale only after the first mortgage had been fully paid. Many lenders will not offer second mortgages, insisting instead on firsts only.

SREA

An acronym for Society of Real Estate Appraisers. This is a professional association to which qualified appraisers can belong. Whenever you hire an appraiser you are encouraged to look for the SREA designation.

Subject To

A contingency clause. Also a phrase often used to indicate that a buyer is not assuming the mortgage liability of a seller. For example, if the seller has an assumable loan and you (the buyer) "assumes" the loan, you are taking over liability for payment. On the other hand, if you purchase "subject to" the mortgage, you do not assume liability for payment.

Subordination Clause

A clause that can be inserted into a mortgage document to keep that mortgage secondary to any other mortgages. Mortgages are valued according to the chronological order on which they are put onto a property. The first mortgage on a property is called a "first" in time, the next mortgage is a "second" in time, the next a "third" in time, and so forth. The order is important because in the event of foreclosure, all the money from a foreclosure sale goes to pay off the lender of the first. Only if there is any left over does it then go to pay off the holder of the second. Then any subsequent money left over goes to pay off the lender of the third, and so forth. The earlier the number of the mortgage, the more desirable and the more superior the mortgage is considered.

Normally, when a first mortgage is paid off, the second advances to become the first, the third to the second, and so forth. However, since some lenders only offer first mortgages, having a second advance to the first position could prevent you from refinancing with a new first (unless the second and other inferior mortgages were fully paid off). This you might not want to do.

Hence, a subordination clause can be inserted into the second and other inferior mortgages. It specifies that the mortgage will remain in its current position, thus allowing you to pay off the existing first and get a new first.

This is a technique used by developers who give the sellers of land a second mortgage and then get a new first for construction. Today, most institutional lenders either will not allow a subordination clause inserted in any second or inferior mortgage they make; or if they do subordinate, they will limit the amount of the first.

Title

This is evidence that you actually have the right of ownership of real property. It is in the form of a deed (there are many different types of deeds) that specifies the kind of title you have (joint, common, or other).

Title Insurance Policy

This is an insurance policy that covers the title to your home. It may list you or the lender as a beneficiary. The title insurance policy is issued by a title insurance company or through an attorney under-written by an insurance company. It specifies that if for any covered reason your title is defective, the company will correct the title or pay you up to a specified amount, usually the amount of the purchase price or the mortgage.

Before issuing such a policy, for which either the buyer or the seller or both (as determined by local custom) must pay a fee, the title insurance company investigates the chain of title and notifies all parties of any defects, such as liens. These must then be paid off. Sometimes if it is not desirable to pay them off (as in the case of old bonds), a policy of title insurance with an exception may be issued.

Most states have standard title insurance policies. For example, California has a CLTA, or policy approved by the California Land Title Association. It may not be a very complete policy and may not give you total coverage. A more complete policy is the ALTA, defined earlier in this appendix.

VA Loan

A mortgage guaranteed by the Veterans Administration. The VA actually only guarantees a small percentage of the amount loaned, but since it guarantees the first monies loaned, lenders are willing to accept it. In a VA loan the government advances no money; rather, the mortgage is made by a private lender such as a bank.

Wraparound Financing

Here a lender blends two mortgages. If the lender is a seller, then he or she doesn't receive all cash. However, instead of simply giving the buyer–borrower a simple second mortgage, the lender combines the balance due on an existing mortgage (usually an existing first) with an additional loan.

Thus the wrap includes both the second and the first. The borrower makes payments to the lender, who then keeps part of the payment and in turn makes payments on the existing mortgage.

The wrap is used typically by a seller who either doesn't trust the buyer to make payments on a first or who wants to get a higher interest rate.

Index